This Is the Day

By Bruce Green

Published by
Spiritbuilding Publishers
9700 Ferry Road, Waynesville, Ohio 45068

THIS IS THE DAY
By Bruce Green

ISBN: 978–1–96480–506–1

Spiritbuilding
PUBLISHERS

spiritbuilding.com

Contents

Dedications

To Kevin Pfalser, David Janagin, and David Bogard—
Good friends who have been a blessing to me over the years.

Special Thanks

To *Janice Green, Alison James,* and *Chris Tidwell* for their generosity of time in reading this and offering their invaluable insights. To *Laura Green* for her work as my unfailing creative consultant and sounding board.

Foreword

"Teach us to number our days, that we may gain a heart of wisdom."
(Psalm 90:12)

2 7,905—that is our life expectancy in terms of days, according to the CDC's National Center for Health Statistics. That sounds like a lot of days, and yet, which one of us hasn't experienced the feeling of looking back and wondering where the time went? For most of us, the frequency of this feeling only increases with age.

That being so, is there any way we can get some traction regarding time and how quickly it seems to be passing? The answer involves good news and not-so-good news. The not-so-good first: there is no way to pause time, slow it down, or manipulate it in any fashion. It is the steadiest of stable forces God has created in our universe. However, the good news is there is a way we can experience time more powerfully, appreciate it more fully, and remember it with more bliss.

What is it?

The answer is so simple you might be skeptical: we learn to approach time and life as they are given to us by God in that marvelous 24-hour increment we refer to as a day. While this answer might be easy to understand, translating it into reality is a greater challenge. Many of us have lifestyles that aren't particularly conducive to life on these terms. Many live at breakneck speed where the days blur by like lines on the highway. Others live in anticipation of some future event—the present is merely an obstacle they want to get around as quickly as possible. Then, there are those who are trapped in the past. Rather than viewing each day as a cause for celebration, they are used merely to contrast with how things used to be.

Time, life, and opportunity all intersect in the special moment known as *today.* If experience teaches us anything, it is that life isn't forever and can be, at times, quite fragile. We can be here one day and gone the next. Learning to live within a day should be the goal for all of us. And while it is true we hear a great deal about "living in the moment," "living for today," and similar expressions, we hear precious little about the Christ who makes it all possible. Let me just say on the front end that if Jesus isn't involved in our daily lives, then being the best version of ourselves and maximizing our time and lives is just wishful thinking on our part. For it was He who said, "I have come that they may have life, and have it abundantly" (John 10:10 ESV; see also 20:30–31).

Ultimately, that is what we're interested in, isn't it?

Introduction

Have you ever wondered what life was like for Lazarus *the morning after* he was raised from the dead? This would be after he woke up, pinched himself, and realized it wasn't all a dream—he had been dead, and now he was alive! What happened next? (After all, it wasn't like he had anything on his calendar since he had been dead the past four days).

There is nothing in the gospels concerning the matter, so it is all conjecture—but aren't you curious as to what kind of thoughts raced through his mind? Whatever else was true, I can't imagine life could be the same for him. I'm not saying that because I think pre-death Lazarus was a slacker of any kind—after all, he was a follower and a close friend of Jesus— but coming back from the dead would change everything, wouldn't it? From my perspective, a couple of things would have popped into his mind almost immediately.

First, he would have recognized, in a way that most of us cannot, that he had absolutely nothing to fear. After all, he had been to death and back, so a lot of the issues that tend to warp our wheels wouldn't even register with him. Then, as a disciple of Jesus, I'm guessing he doubled down on his commitment to live with vision, passion, and purpose. After all, he understood and appreciated the reality of death and, consequently, the urgency of life.

There would be one more challenge facing Lazarus—how to live this way *each day*. The first day wouldn't be a problem. The first couple of weeks were probably a piece of cake. But after a while, the days would become less distinguishable and start to blend into each other. Lazarus would notice he was not quite as sensitive to and aware of all that was going on around him— the edges of his life had somehow become dulled. Before long, the one who had experienced the circle of life would find himself being worn down by the cycle of life. The one who returned from the grave would be struggling against the swirling gnats of routine, tedium, and monotony. They weren't like the sickness that had taken his life, but they certainly threatened the fullness of it.

If you belong to Jesus Christ, you've returned from the dead (Ephesians 2:1ff). You were raised up with Christ by the grace of God, and life can never be the same!

But like Lazarus in our hypothetical example, we can be ground down by the sameness of days and the flatness of the landscape around us. We face the same challenge of learning how to live within each day for the Lord. We want to, as David Brooks says in *The Second Mountain*, "lead the kind of life that keeps [our] heart and soul awake every day." Although Brooks was talking about making a wise vocational choice, his words speak to the passion disciples desire to have in pursuing their calling (see Ephesians 4:1ff, 5:1ff). Anne Morrow Lindbergh captured it in her classic, *Gift from the Sea* when she wrote, "I want a singleness of eye, a purity of intention, a central core to my life that will enable me to live out . . . [my] obligations and activities as well as I can."

But how do we do that? Is there a checklist to follow? Are there routines to implement (or avoid)?

Unfortunately, there is no book in the Bible called "Living as a daily disciple." The Scripture isn't put together that way. It is a collection of historical books, prophetical pieces, occasional letters, poetry, prayers, and songs written over the centuries. There is very little systematic arrangement or attempts to speak exhaustively on subjects. It is designed to be read and re-read, pored over and prayed over, discussed and debated—interacted with in such a way that its teachings are caught as much as they are taught. It is the living word from a living God.

My purpose in this book is to walk us through the holy ground of Scripture as we think about what it means to live within a day for Jesus. I have no doubts that my reach exceeds my grasp in many places, but I do believe you'll find some solid principles that will keep you moving daily in heaven's direction.

May God richly bless you as you live for Him.

Thinking About a Day

"Set wide the window. Let me drink in the day"
Edith Wharton

In the Beginning

(The design of a day)

"Everything is as it should be. God's creation is perfect."
Yasmin Mogahed

What is a day? In scientific terms, it is the amount of time it takes our planet to rotate on its axis. This means that there is a cycle of daylight and darkness each day. The daytime generally corresponds with activities, and the nighttime with rest and sleep. When we wake again, it is the beginning of another day. You could look at it like we live, die (sleep), and are reborn with each new day. It is a little lifetime all its own, with a beginning, middle, and end.

If you are paying attention (and especially if you already have the idea in mind), it is not hard to conclude that what we refer to as a day was designed by God with humanity in mind. In the translation I'm using (NIV), we're only 66 words into Genesis before we come across this word being used to describe the portion of the day when it is light outside (1:5). If we continue just a little farther to the 83rd word, we find it again—this time being used to refer to the 24-hour period consisting of both darkness and light (also v. 5). In response to creation, the Hebrews marked their day as beginning at sundown rather than midnight as we do.

This means that, like everything else, days don't exist independently of God. When our Father made the material world, He also created the dimension of time for us to live in (v. 3–5).

A day is the most basic unit of time created by God. Hours, minutes, and seconds are all ideas we came up with. While they are good and useful in their own way, they can also distract us from appreciating a day as the most significant measurement of time. After all, there is *daily bread, taking up our cross each day,* and serving a God *who daily bears our burdens* (Psalm 68:19). Paul wrote about our *daily life* winning the respect of outsiders (1 Thessalonians 4:12), while the writer of Hebrews mentioned encouraging one another *daily* (3:13). It is hard to get away from the idea that in terms of time, the currency God favors is the one He created.

The word "day" occurs 11 times in Genesis 1 and occupies a pivotal but often overlooked aspect of the creation account. (The exception to this would be when people are debating the length of a creation day, which I have no desire to do. Since we're not told otherwise and the context does not necessitate it, I take "day" to be a regular, 24-hour day as we know it).

Moving past the creation of a day, we are introduced to another intriguing truth: God chose to create the universe in six days. If you think about it, He could have accomplished what He did over any amount of time or in no amount of time, but He purposely chose to do it over six days. Though our attention is usually drawn to all the marvelous things God made, we seldom consider He also had in mind how He wanted to bring everything into being—one day at a time.

As we read Genesis 1, one of the things that stands out is the peaceful, purposeful rhythm of the narrative. You don't get the sense there was any hurry or worry in God's creative work. It was as paced as it was powerful— we hear of evenings and mornings and goodness as regularly as if they were water lapping up on the shoreline. There was no anxious wringing of hands because so much more needed to be done. God was quite content and at peace with His work each day. The day was filled with creating, and when it was done, it was done.

Why did God choose to do things this way? Why isn't life just one big, long day? What prompted Him to make a day just 24 hours long? There are a couple of texts that provide some insight into our attempt to answer these questions.

Exodus 20:8–11

In this passage, God was speaking through Moses to the Israelites at Mt. Sinai after He had delivered them from years of suffering and oppression in Egypt. He had told them of His desire for them to be "a kingdom of priests and a holy nation" (19:6). To that end, He gave them what is known in Hebrew as the "ten words" (see 34:28), which were representative of the fuller law He would reveal to them. In v. 8, they were told to "Remember the Sabbath day by keeping it holy." The passage goes on to say in v. 11, "For in six days the Lord made the heavens and the earth, the sea, and all that is in them, but He rested on the seventh day." The idea is that as God worked for six days in creating everything and then "rested" on the seventh (i.e., ceased from creating), the Israelites should work for six days and rest on the seventh day.

While initially this text looks like more of a reason for resting (and working) than explaining to us why God made a unit of time known as a day, there's more to it than that. In doing His creative work and resting in the way He did, God modeled how humanity would image Him. And the fact that He chose to do it in days tells us that He made them with us in mind. In the six days of creation and the day of rest, God not only provided the model for our work and leisure but also the basic framework for our lives.

Mark 2:27

We see this idea reinforced when we move forward to Jesus' statement that "The Sabbath was made for man, not man for the Sabbath" (Mark 2:27). The Pharisees were sure things were the other way around—that man had been made to keep the Sabbath. From there, they devised an excessive list of what people could and couldn't do on that day. As a result, the Sabbath became a crushing burden rather than the blessing God had intended it to be. (Religion always goes wrong when man over-involves himself and under-involves God).

Jesus' words were intended to reverse this situation by correcting their misunderstanding of the Sabbath's design. For our purposes, we need to see that what God made for man was more than just the principle of rest—specifically, it was *a 24-hour* rest period. You can't say the Sabbath day was made for humanity without also affirming the more fundamental truth that days were created with us in mind. From these two passages, it is clear that a day is not something that arbitrarily pops up in the creation account—God designed it with us in mind.

What This Means for Us

If, in a day, we have an important part of God's framework for living rather than a random unit of time, then part of appreciating and honoring it means we make sure we work within God's design rather than against it. Most of us have had the experience of using something incorrectly: driving with the parking brake on, using a shoe for a hammer, or a dime for a screwdriver. I was once pulled over by a state trooper who thought I wasn't wearing my seat belt. It looked that way to him because instead of the strap going over my shoulder as it was supposed to, I had it under my arm. When he saw that I did have my belt on, he pointed out that if I were in an accident, it wouldn't work as intended because I wasn't wearing it as it was designed to be used.

How we look at a day can be a lot like that. We have the choice of ignoring its framework or using it as it is intended. If we choose to ignore it, then like the seat belt, it won't benefit us in the way God desires. But if we choose to honor the design of a day, we will find ourselves blessed and in harmony with God's will as expressed through creation.

The word becoming flesh: Challenge yourself to find the rhythm of living within a single day. To help you do this, determine if you are more of a macro person (you take a more extensive approach to life, such as a work week or whole week) or a micro person (you approach life in smaller segments like morning, afternoon, evening, or even a few hours at a time). Determining this will help you know which direction you need to go in.

The Undervalued Asset

"Nothing is to be rated higher than the value of the day."
Johann Wolfgang Von Goethe

I t was being stored inside a shoe box in the attic—a porcelain vase embellished with exquisite artwork. It was part of the estate she had received from her grandparents. They had inherited it from an uncle, who had acquired it in the late 19th century. The woman who owned the vase didn't care for it any more than her grandparents had, but she thought there was a possibility it might have some value. Rather than relegating it to more years in the attic, she stuffed some newspaper into the box to protect the vase, took the train, then the metro, and finally walked the remaining distance to the Paris Sotheby's. There, the 30 cm vase was identified as belonging to the Qing Dynasty and was estimated to have been made between 1735 and 1795. It was subsequently put up for auction and sold for about 19 million dollars—not a bad return for something previously unable to earn its way out of the attic!

It is easy for us to think about a day the way the owner thought of the vase—we believe there is some value to it, but we seriously underestimate just how much that is. As a result, we can be pretty blasé about a day. We put it in a shoe box and store it away in the attic of our mind. After all, we are confident there are plenty more where it came from, so there's no reason to get overly excited about it.

One of the ways the biblical witness confronts us is in regard to our thinking. By this, I mean that our basic understanding and perception of reality is challenged in numerous ways because God doesn't think the way we do (Isaiah 55:8–9). Therefore, as He reveals His thoughts to us, we often have to restructure ours because while He sees things as they are, we tend to see them as we are. For many of us, this is true regarding the value (or the lack of it) we assign to a day.

What Makes a Day Valuable?

When we think about a day and what makes it valuable, it can be appraised in a couple of ways. The first is in accordance with its *relative* value. That simply means a day is important because of what it relates to: your birthday, your anniversary, or some other memorable occasion. It could be something you're looking forward to, like the first day of vacation, the day you close on your house, or a trip you've planned. It could even be something as simple as the weather, which is supposed to be nice enough for you to be able to spend time outside. Whatever it is, relative value is when we appraise a day based on something attached to it.

The other reason a day is precious is its *inherent* value. This means we are valuing the day for itself—a 24-hour period given to us to make of it what we are able, with God's help. In this regard, it is like a hundred-dollar bill. A hundred-dollar bill can be clean or dirty, new or old, crisp or crumpled, and it is still worth the same thing—one hundred dollars. That is the inherent value of the bill. The same thing is true of a day. Each day has an inherent value equal to every other day. In this sense, days don't have quality (that's a relative value); they simply have quantity, and each day is the same (i.e., each day exists as an independent and complete entity).

I think I speak for most people when I say it is our default setting to value days more for their relative worth rather than their intrinsic value. We tend to love Saturdays and Sundays because they are part of the weekend, and for most of us, that means no work (or school) and the freedom to do more of what we enjoy doing. While there's nothing wrong and much that's right in celebrating a day because of its relative worth, there is also something potentially hazardous associated with it.

What is it? In valuing a particular day because of its relative worth, we will devalue or even trivialize the days that come before or after it. Let's go back to the weekend. We all get excited about it—but who gets excited about Monday? For most people, it is a day they just try to get through because its relative value is often thought of negatively—it is the first day after the weekend. It means going back to the grind of work or school. It is a day to be endured rather than enjoyed.

By consciously or unconsciously assigning any day a negative value, we completely ignore its intrinsic worth. That's a fundamentally flawed perspective, and not surprisingly, it leads to a muddled approach to life. Okay, so Monday is the first day of the work week, and we'd rather be at home than at work or school. Does that mean the day is without value? Of course not. If we return to our hundred-dollar bill illustration, maybe Monday is a bit crumpled up, but it still has the same value as any other day.

And what exactly is that?

Given by God

When thinking about what makes a day valuable, the place to start is by recognizing that it is something given to us by God. We have no power to create one. God has enabled humanity to do many extraordinary things— split the atom, map the human genome, and invent something like the James Webb Space Telescope. However, we don't have the ability to go into the laboratory and create a batch of days. In fact, we can't come up with even one. Days are part of God's creative domain, not ours.

Our Father gives us each day, but He doesn't send down two or three years' worth at a time for us to stockpile; in His wisdom, He provides them to us one at a time. We have absolutely no guarantee of anything other than the day we're living in. Tomorrow might come for us, or it might not—we don't know. What we do know is that every day we receive is a gift from Him.

Unique

A day is like a fingerprint or a snowflake—no two are exactly alike. Maybe we should think of each one as having its own DNA. Whatever metaphor we choose, the truth is that a day cannot be replaced and will not be replicated. That alone should sensitize us to appreciate each day for what it is rather than merely seeing it as a stepping-stone to the weekend or whatever it is we're anticipating. It is the creation of God, and we honor that by treating each day in a way that reflects its uniqueness.

My wife and I were at a yogurt shop where a picture promoting the peach yogurt she later enjoyed noted it was "available for a limited time only." The phrase could have been employed for several reasons. Maybe the company was testing the product's sales potential and wanted to get feedback (like when a movie is test-marketed). The yogurt could have been seasonal, or their supply was limited by some other factor. From a cynical point of view, I suppose the phrase could have been used to create a scarcity mindset in hopes of boosting sales.

Whatever the truth was, the greater truth is that everything in this life is available "for a limited time only." Sunsets, the laughter of children, rich friendships—none of these come with a guarantee of tomorrow. Everything about life as we know it is ours for a limited time only. Children grow up, and friendships can fade due to time, distance, or death. There will never be another day exactly like the one you are experiencing. We appreciate that each day is one-of-a-kind by not taking any of them for granted.

Alive with Possibilities

Because every day is a unique blessing from our Father's gracious hand, each one has the same intrinsic value: it is priceless. One reason it is invaluable is because it is alive with possibilities. It might be a Monday, but something could happen that might change the rest of your life—or you could do something that could change someone else's life. The truth is, we don't know. The only thing we can be sure of is every day represents 24 hours of God-given potential.

There was a sale going on at the store. There were bags and several tables of designated merchandise. The object was to get as much merchandise into a bag as possible. The price for each bag was the same no matter how many items were in it. The same principle holds true in regard to each day God gives us. We must fill it with as much as possible because anything less is a wasted opportunity.

Putting it all together, God has given us this special, priceless present known as today so that *with* Him, we will make something of it *for* Him. To do this, we must make sure we do more than value certain days—we must appreciate the precious and original qualities of each and every one.

It takes some discipline to change our way of thinking and to adapt our lifestyle. It is not unlike when the electricity goes out, and we have to remind ourselves to quit flicking the light switch when walking into a room. We have to make a mental checklist of the things that will not function (the router, television, chargers, etc.) and adjust our behavior. The good news is that God created us to be adaptable when we put our minds to it, so once we switch over to a no-electricity frame of mind, we're okay (assuming the electricity doesn't stay off too long!).

Don't undervalue what God has given to you in the gift of a day. It is an invaluable, never-to-be-repeated collection of moments, alive with possibilities. It is fashionable to talk about how we spend a day, but we're better off thinking about it as something we invest in. This is what it means to be a disciple of Jesus.

The word becoming flesh: Take some time toward the end of the day to review its events, making sure to note the blessings you experienced. A journal will be helpful for some, while others will find sharing it with someone or perhaps praying about it works well for them.

Carpe Diem

"Seize the moment.
Man was never intended to become an oyster."
Teddy Roosevelt

Something About the Book of Ecclesiastes

Ecclesiastes is like your favorite chewy food because it only yields many of its benefits after you've worked with it for a while. As others have noted, there is something fitting about a book dealing with many of life's difficulties being itself difficult. The style fits the subject matter.

I've come to view the book as being much like another wisdom book—Job. That book relates how, in the midst of his horrific suffering and losses (1:1—2:10), Job had three friends who came to offer their sympathy and support to him. During their visit, they engaged in extended conversations regarding their perception and understanding of life (primarily as it related to Job's circumstances). Some of what they said is accurate, but much isn't. God set everything straight at the end of the book (chapters 38—42).

For those who wonder how a book containing so many things that weren't true could be inspired by God to be part of Scripture, think about Satan's statement in Genesis 3:4 or other falsehoods recorded throughout Scripture (Genesis 12:10–13, 20:1–2, 26:7 and plenty of other places). What is true is people thought, spoke, and acted on these words even though they were incorrect. God wanted them to be part of the biblical witness so we could learn from negative examples as well as positive ones (2 Timothy 3:16–17).

Following Dillard & Longman III (*An Introduction to the Old Testament*) and Shepherd (*The Expositor's Bible Commentary*), I think we're to look at Ecclesiastes in much the same manner as Job. The main section of the book (from 1:2—12:8) features the teachings of someone known in Hebrew as Qoheleth (koh hel' ith) and translated as "the Teacher" or "the Preacher," depending on the version you're using. Like Job and his friends, he shares his perspective on life. While there are nuggets of truth in his words that can easily be overlooked and under-appreciated (3:11, 4:9–12, 5:5–7, 10), there are also many areas where he goes off the rails (1:2,14, 2:17–23, 3:18–21).

The writer of the book, who introduces Qoheleth in 1:1, begins his conclusion in 12:9 as he speaks to someone he calls "my son" (v. 12), who could be just that, or it could be a figure of speech for a student or disciple. Whatever the case might be, the writer has presented Qoheleth's teaching to him, which is representative of what he refers to as "the words of the wise" and "their collected sayings" (v. 11). He commends Qoheleth's efforts and intent ("The Preacher sought to find delightful words and write words of truth correctly," v. 10 NASB). Qoheleth and others like him share words that are painful (v. 11). They are also plentiful ("and further, from these, my son, be warned" v. 12, *Young's Literal Translation),* so much so that you could easily spend the rest of your life studying such things and, in the end, have little more than exhaustion to show for it.

Rather than being overwhelmed by such speculative wisdom (see 1Corinthians 1:21), it is better to anchor in God's revelation and find meaning and purpose by following Him (Ecclesiastes 12:13–14). This conclusion comes from and points to the Torah (see Deuteronomy 6:1–2) in contrast to the "words of the wise" (Ecclesiastes 12:7). It is worlds away from Qoheleth's take of everything being "meaningless"—something he asserts 35 times throughout the book, finishing with a trifecta in v. 8. Just as God set everything straight at the end of Job, the writer of Ecclesiastes does the same as he points us to revering the Lord and walking in obedience to His commands.

The Carpe Diem Passages

These are the texts in Ecclesiastes where the writer encourages us to make the most of life here and now: 2:24–25, 3:12–13, 22, 5:18–20, 8:15, 9:7–10. They are usually viewed from one of two perspectives depending on what you understand the book's overall thrust to be. If you believe Qoheleth is writing to tell people how to have joy in life, then you will probably see these texts as the mountaintops of a book depicting an otherwise bleak existence. If you understand the book as chronicling Qoheleth's fruitless search for meaning in life through his own wisdom, then they come across as a consolation prize in his failed mission.

Although, at present, I view Ecclesiastes more from the second perspective, the carpe diem passages contain kernels of truth for us if we are willing to hear them and work with them. They need to be distilled from Qoheleth's jaded perspective. For example, note how, in the last of these passages, he tells us to "Enjoy life with your wife, whom you love, all the days of this meaningless life that God has given you under the sun—all your meaningless days. For this is your lot in life and in your toilsome labor under the sun" (9:9). That's not really anyone's idea of a big finish—except maybe Qoheleth's. Still, there is treasure to be found.

One jewel is that he attributes finding joy with recognizing life is a gift God gives us to enjoy. This principle is present in all the *carpe diem* passages. It is also found in 1 Timothy 6:17, where Paul speaks of "God, who richly provides us with everything for our enjoyment." There's more to all these texts, of course, but what I want to work with is the basic truth that life is a gift from God, and we honor Him by finding joy in that gift.

The first part—that life (i.e., food, work, possessions, marriage, family, etc.) is an endowment from God—is a truth most of us accept in a generalized way, as when we give thanks before a meal. That is good as far as it goes, but we don't want to be like Qoheleth, who doesn't seem to take this truth far enough.

God deserves more than a generalized "thank You" for all He does. Paul quoted the Cretan writer Epimenides to the effect that "in Him we live and move and have our being" (Acts 17:28). In 1 Corinthians 4:7, he reduced it down to two questions, "What do you have that you did not receive? And if you did receive it, why do you boast as if you did not?" Jesus spoke of God sending sunshine and rain to all (Matthew 5:45—a much different take than Qoheleth's in 1:5–8). He also taught about God's involvement with the birds of the air and flowers of the field and how they demonstrate His care for people, who are "much more valuable" (6:26–28). God's hand touches our lives daily in more ways than we can enumerate or understand. To live well is to recognize and live with an ever-deepening appreciation of our Father's blessings.

However, Qoheleth wants us to do more than simply acknowledge God's gifts—he wants us to find joy in them. While it is true that "God gives . . . the ability to enjoy them" (5:19), it is equally true that we have the choice of whether or not we will embrace this attitude. This is the assumption behind all the carpe diem texts. How do we find joy in God's blessings? There is more to this than we might initially think. We only fully experience joy when we have learned to receive God's gifts for what they are—not over-analyzing them or trying to leverage them into something bigger, better, or longer lasting. In other words, we receive them like a child (Mark 10:15).

God's Gift of Today

This is easiest to see in the treasure of today. In the previous chapter, we talked about seeing each day as a gift from God, but we're moving a step beyond that now as we think about finding joy in that gift. I imagine we've all had the experience of receiving a present that . . . well, let's just say we were grateful for the intent of the giver, their thoughtfulness, and generosity. Still, we never really enjoyed the present (it didn't fit, wouldn't work, or we already had one). In the same way, we can be grateful for God's gift of a day but fail to find joy in it.

To find joy in the treasure of a day, we must learn to see it for what it is—a limited but priceless period of time and opportunity. It is not to be spent looking back at yesterday or being preoccupied with tomorrow. We won't assume the blessing of today means we have tomorrow promised because we don't. Instead, we will invest it by focusing on the present and whatever it holds. Often, we fail to appreciate something until after it is gone. In regard to a day, we must not wait for experience to teach us at the end of our lives what education can teach us right now. Approaching life with this mindset frees us to receive, celebrate, and enjoy a day for the gift that it is.

Finally, to move well past Qoheleth, we not only honor God by recognizing each day as a blessing from Him and finding joy in it, but we ultimately honor Him by loving Him with all our heart, soul, mind, and strength. We enjoy the gift, but we love the Giver! Again, it shouldn't be assumed that this is always a natural, easy progression. Our growth can be stunted, and as a result, we love our gifts and live for them rather than the God who supplies them. We can make our marriage, our family, our job, or something else the center of our life rather than Him.

This appears to have been the stumbling block for the rich young ruler (Matthew 19:16ff). He had been blessed by God in many ways, but when Christ called on him to sell his possessions and give the money to the poor—he was unable to do it. He was more attached to his blessings than he was to the One who provided him those blessings. We should be hesitant to sit in judgment on him since we have not been commanded to do what he was, but we can learn from him and remind ourselves that the most authentic joy comes not from our gifts but from a relationship with the One who gives them.

Ecclesiastes and Qoheleth start us down a road that ultimately results in us slowing down, simplifying, and looking up. We learn to look at life overall, and each day in particular, as a distinctive treasure given to us by God for our enjoyment. And if we carry all of this to its logical conclusion, we recognize that even greater than the gifts is the Giver of them.

The word becomes flesh: Lean into the joyful moments of each day. If it involves others (and it usually will), say something to them about the specialness of it. It can be as simple as "I enjoyed talking/visiting with you." Acknowledging it to our Father in prayer (silent or spoken) is also helpful and healthy.

Thinking About Daily Discipleship

*"Relying on God has to begin all over again every day
as if nothing had yet been done."*
C.S. Lewis

Something About the Word "Daily"

Isuppose there's some risk in using the word *daily* in connection with our discipleship (even though the Scripture freely does so). The word could be understood as it is when taking medication daily—we get it over with first thing in the morning, so we don't have to think about it the rest of the day. That's clearly not the intent of the word in discipleship texts. Another possibility is that *daily* could be taken to mean adopting a checklist mentality in an effort to control the day. Of course, God controls the day, not us. What we control is whether or not we want to recognize that and give the day to Him. As to the matter of checklists, if life were that simple, you can be sure the Scripture would have such a list. The fact that it doesn't should steer us away from such an approach to life.

How, then, can we understand the Scripture's employment of the word *daily* in passages relating to discipleship? To begin with, rather than assigning the word a uniform meaning, *daily* should be understood according to the context of each passage. For example, the "daily bread" of Matthew 6:11 has to do with the day's provisions—a 24-hour period. The word is used in its most common, basic sense. In Hebrews 3:13, such a definition is functional, but it doesn't bring out the fullness of the writer's plea. Opportunity is foremost in his mind (as made clear by the phrase "as long as it is called 'Today'"). He is saying, "Take advantage of your *daily opportunities* to encourage each other." The word has an added dimension here and isn't being used exactly as it is in the "daily bread" text. They're in the same house but not the same room, and recognizing this brings richness and depth to our understanding of the text.

What is true in all our texts is that daily carries the idea of something that is a consistent practice or attitude. And as such, it is an expression of where our heart is. When we're told to "pray without ceasing"—that's obviously not literal. But it does mean that we adopt the attitude of prayer regarding the whole of life. There is no occasion where prayer isn't vital. I think the word *daily* points us in a similar direction. These things become part of our regular life to the point that they are more than *what* we do—they become *who* we are.

When we consider *daily* from this vantage point more than a frequency perspective, it has a deeper, character-related meaning that is consistent with its discipleship usage. This is helpful to keep in mind as we encounter the different daily aspects of following Jesus. God is not giving us a checklist to follow; He wants to transform our hearts and lives for kingdom living!

Daily Rejoicing

This is the day that the Lord has made;
let us rejoice and be glad in it.
(Psalm 118:24 ESV)

Most of us are quite familiar with this verse. We've read it, heard it quoted, possibly sang it, and many of us have the impression it means something like *God made today, so we should celebrate it.* That's not a bad or unbiblical thought, but it is not exactly what the psalmist had in mind either.

A Look at Psalm 118

Psalm 118 begins and ends with "Give thanks to the Lord, for He is good; His love endures forever" (v. 1, 29 NIV). Whenever we find a chapter or section of Scripture bracketed in this way (sometimes referred to as an *inclusio*), it is a good indicator that what lies in between is an expansion on the words that introduce and conclude it. This is certainly true of Psalm 118. It extols God's love (*hesed*) and calls for His covenant people to join in the profession and celebration of it.

The psalm is part of what is known as the *Hallel* (Psalms 113—118). *Hallel* means "praise," and these six psalms were commonly recited at the annual feasts and on other joyous occasions. Many scholars think the *Hallel* was what Jesus and His disciples sang after celebrating Passover (Matthew 26:30).

The psalm appears to have been written for some form of temple procession (see vv. 19–21, 26–27). Because of this, it probably makes more sense to hear it as Israel celebrating Yahweh's rescue of the nation (see vv. 2–4) rather than reflecting the writer's personal situation. Additionally, v. 14 is a quote from a song celebrating Israel's deliverance from Egypt (Exodus 15:2), while vv. 17–18 refers to the nation's exile in Babylon.

Viewing the psalm from a national perspective provides a pointed context for vv. 22–24. The stone the builders rejected would be Israel—rejected first by the Egyptians and then the Babylonians, but nonetheless brought out of their bondage to become the cornerstone of God's plans for the future. "The Lord has done this, and it is marvelous in our eyes" (v. 23). Indeed, it is.

The Psalm Applied to Jesus

But there's more. The New Testament writers repeatedly appropriate this passage to Jesus (see Matthew 21:42; Mark 12:10; Luke 20:17; Acts 4:11; Ephesians 2:20; 1 Peter 2:7). Like Israel, He experienced rejection. As with Israel, Yahweh reversed the course of events so that Christ became the cornerstone of His plan for the world.

"This is the day the Lord has made; let us rejoice and be glad in it." As followers of God did in ancient times, we celebrate the deliverance that God brought at the Red Sea and in returning the nation from captivity. These are historical out-workings of His goodness and reminders of His enduring love. But as we have seen from its usage in the NT, this psalm speaks to us of more than the exodus or the return from exile—it forecasts the rejection of the Messiah as well as the reversal God would bring about through Jesus' resurrection.

Peter connects these two things in Acts 4 when he says, "It is by the name of Jesus Christ of Nazareth, whom you crucified but whom God raised from the dead, that this man stands before you healed. Jesus is 'the stone the builders rejected, which has become the cornerstone'" (v. 10–11). In the resurrection, God reversed the world's verdict of rejection and declared Jesus to be His Son (Romans 1:4). It is in Jesus' resurrection that the words "This is the day the Lord has made; let us rejoice and be glad in it" find their supreme fulfillment.

What This Means

It would be easy to conclude from the application of Psalm 118 in Acts 4 that what we're called to rejoice in each day is the resurrection of Christ. While that's certainly an important (and needed) perspective, I think the psalm aims at something even more significant and profound. It is suggesting that rather than rejoicing in each day because of the resurrection, we celebrate the day because of the God who brings reversal. Remember, the inclusio is "Give thanks to the Lord, for He is good; His love endures forever." While we are grateful for all three reversals (the exodus, the return from captivity and the resurrection), they all flow from and point us to something of even greater significance that made them all possible—the faithful, loving character of Yahweh.

Understanding this enables disciples to face each day with hope and joy. Moreover, we recognize God's goodness is not a passing phase or based on a mood—it is rooted in His holy character. It is who He is, "and it is marvelous in our eyes." We rejoice in the day because His love endures forever. We rejoice in the day because of everything God has revealed Himself through Jesus to be (John 1:18; 14:8–9).

Gloriously Ever After

But even after we've locked into God's character, rejoicing can still be a challenge at times. In our hearts, we know who God is, but the circumstances of life can pound against this conviction like surf battering the shoreline. Add to this another obstacle—we're often looking for reversal in this lifetime, and many times, that's not meant to be. There are many ways in which none of us will be healed and whole until we are *home!*

After all, reversal didn't occur for our Lord during His earthly life. His life ended in a criminal's death while His mother looked on. His body was then placed in a borrowed tomb. There's nothing in any of that which sounds like triumph. Many of God's people suffered similar terrible experiences (see Hebrews 11:36–38). Understanding that reversal often comes after this life is a necessary step for us to develop the patient endurance needed to deal with our circumstances—even when they are excruciatingly difficult and challenge us to the depth of our being.

The biblical witness provides numerous examples of people living in desperate situations, from Job to Jeremiah to the seven churches of Asia addressed in Revelation. Then there are those disciples we know of today who are traveling down troubled paths. Maybe they are in countries where the Christian faith isn't accepted, and they are experiencing severe persecution and even loss of life. But often, we don't have to look outside our own church family to find people who are up against it in ways that would stagger us. Then there are others we hear about.

Two such disciples are Harrison and Hayley Waldron. On August 14, 2015, fourteen months after they were married, Harrison was involved in an ATV accident and sustained a traumatic brain injury. For three months, he was in a comatose state before he emerged into consciousness. He had significant physical limitations but was fully aware, alert, and living each day for the Lord. Hayley and members of the family provided constant care for Harrison. Life wasn't easy, and each day posed its own challenges. Listen to Hayley's words:

> Sometimes, I look 10 years into the future and wonder where we will be, but there's no guarantee. There's no knowing, which can be a really scary place, but I've gotten used to it. The bottom line is we're going to surrender to this new life and this new plan God has laid before us. This is not what we wanted at all, but sometimes God lets us have these opportunities to glorify him. People always told us that God was going to have a special purpose for us. I was not thinking that this would be what it was. But we know God's got us, and he has great plans for us.

> I'm so happy to be living it for the Lord—even when it hurts. God has done great things in my life, and I know if He loves me and He loves Harrison, which I believe He does tremendously, we're going to be OK. He's going to give us meaning in our brokenness. And one day when we're all completely whole in heaven, it is going to be amazing. I believe we're going to see some fruit from this trial, which is what our lives are all about. It is about getting people to heaven and living this wonderful life for eternity. It is what I signed up for when I gave my life to Christ.

> As for now, we will keep at it. We will count our blessings, and we will see God work in our lives. And when the going gets tough, we'll

help comfort others the way the Lord comforts us, by pointing them to Christ and to the beautiful life God has offered us all. We'll remind them there's more than this and that we have renewed life, light, and love through Jesus both now and forever. We are going to be okay, y'all. We are going to be *more* than okay.

Harrison went to be with the Lord in June of 2022—almost seven years after his accident. Through their example, he and Hayley powerfully remind us that to whatever degree we might "groan inwardly," "our present sufferings are not worthy to be compared with the glory that will be revealed in us" (Romans 8:23, 18). The one who penned these words also knew something about suffering, and now he knows something about glory (Philippians 1:21ff.). One day we will too!

Having a settled conviction about God's character, purpose, and power allows us to frame our day with the peace, contentment, and joy of knowing that no matter what might happen, we know how it will ultimately end. At the beginning and end of each day, the stone will still be rolled away, the tomb empty, and Jesus Lord over all. He is the ever-shining, brilliant Maker of our future who leads and awaits those who wait on God.

This is the perspective we need in our personal lives and to share with a broken and wounded world. They need to hear that while injustice, cruelty, and suffering might appear to have the last word—they don't. It looked exactly that way in Jesus' time when the crowd called for His crucifixion and mocked Him while on the cross—but the resurrection changed everything. If we are going to stand for truth, beauty, and righteousness, we need to have a resurrection supporting us—one that reminds us that God is good and His love endures forever.

This is the day that the Lord has made; let us rejoice and be glad in it!

The word becomes flesh: Living gloriously ever after begins now. It doesn't mean we become stoics who never experience any emotion; it means in good times or bad and everything in between, we allow our faith in God to supply us with our ultimate outlook in life. We don't take our cues from the world (Romans 12:1–2) but from what our Father tells us. Give some thought to what influences and shapes your core attitudes toward life.

Community Watch

But encourage one another daily, as long as it is called "Today," so that none of you may be hardened by sin's deceitfulness.
(Hebrews 3:13)

Our Need for Encouragement

The nearly four-year-old boy was navigating his way down the fence in his backyard. It consisted of vertical slats (think giant Popsicle sticks) held together by three parallel lines of 2 x 4s running horizontally. He had managed to climb up to the second line (about three feet off the ground) while his hands held on to the top of the fence. He was headed down the fence in this manner. It was a slow process and a long fence.

Unknown to him, his dad watched from a distance but decided to let the situation play out to see how his son handled it. When the boy reached the end of the fence and climbed down, he told him what a great job he had done, and they decided his mom needed to see it. He started down the fence again, but his strength was fading fast. About halfway through, he called his dad over and said, "When I get close to the end, do you think you and Mom could start cheering and clapping for me?"

We all need encouragement, don't we?

Imagine for a moment what your life would be like if you weren't part of a community of faith. You still held to all the beliefs and behaviors you do now, but the difference was that you held them *alone*—in isolation from any other disciples.

While it is difficult for us to grasp exactly what that would be like (as most hypothetical situations are), our imaginations can provide an accurate enough picture to understand that such an existence would be bleak and troubling. Having experienced the richness and blessing of being part of the community of faith, life without that would be lonely and stifling.

During the stay-at-home phase of the pandemic, when we weren't coming together as a church, we had a taste of such isolation. Even though we could communicate through phone calls and various forms of media, we all struggled, some quite severely, with our inability to have face-to-face interaction. I sent daily messages to our members about "the wilderness" we were traveling through and encouraged them to respond. One of them, Kati, wrote the following,

When one has been without food for a while, there is an empty, gnawing feeling in the body . . . There is a hunger in my soul that will not be satisfied until I can once again meet with my church family . . . I want to experience the love that envelops me like a coat on a cold day.

The pandemic underscored our need for community—not the virtual kind with "friends" and "followers," but the face-to-face, flesh-and-blood variety where you can touch, interact, and be much more spontaneous than any screen allows. We need this because community is more than a good idea— it's God's idea. It is where the best in each of us is made better by the best in all of us.

Help from Hebrews

As the letter's name suggests, the recipients were Jewish people who had embraced Jesus as the promised Messiah. They weren't new in their faith (5:11–12), and as can sometimes happen, they seemed to have lost much of the enthusiasm and joy they once had (10:32ff.). To borrow from the letter, they were struggling to stay in the race (12:1ff.). It appears the pressure being placed upon them by family, friends, and peers to renege on their commitment to Jesus and return to strictly Jewish ways (10:19ff. & 25ff.) was wearing them down (6:11–12, 10:36–39, 12:1–13). Considering all this, it is not surprising they needed encouragement, and the writer provides that in the letter (see 13:22 and the dozen "let us" passages where he encourages them in very specific ways). That they were told to encourage each other is something we might not have seen coming (3:13, 10:25).

The Greek word that is translated "encourage" in these two texts is *parakaleo*. It is a compound word with *para* meaning "alongside, beside, near" and *kaleo* meaning "to call." Together, they convey the idea of calling someone to your side when you wish to speak to them in a more intimate and personal way. The context conveys the exact nature of what is said to them. In our two passages, it is clear that it is meant to lend support and lift up, so the translators have chosen the word "encourage" to convey this.

To encourage is to give "support, confidence or hope to someone." Online Etymology traces the word back to the early 15th-century French word *encoragier*, which is a compound of *en* ("make, put in") and *corage* ("courage, heart"). To encourage then, is to put courage or heart in someone!

This brings an important truth to the forefront—it takes courage to live as a disciple of Jesus. Whether you were a first-century Jewish disciple struggling through the circumstances addressed in the Hebrew letter or a 21st-century follower trying to live one day at a time for Christ, we all face challenges that tempt us toward paths of lesser resistance. For disciples of all times, living with courage means embracing difficulty, hardship, and even suffering in order to honor Him who knew all of that and more for us. And one day, when we see Him, absolutely no one will regret any of the brave choices they made for Him.

We need courage, and God supplies us with it through His Spirit (2 Timothy 1:7; Romans 8:15ff.). He also provides it through His word (Hebrews 12:5) and the promises found there (6:13–18). But we also need the bravery that can only come from interacting with other flesh-and-blood followers who are in the arena of conflict with us. Returning to the Hebrew writer's call, we need to be actively involved in instilling courage in others and not be satisfied with simply being on the receiving end of it. We need to do for them what Jonathan did for David in his time of need when he "helped him find strength in God" (1 Samuel 23:16).

There's something about encouraging others that brings out the best in us. It is almost impossible to provide spiritual first aid, a booster shot, or, in extreme cases, CPR to someone else without receiving benefits ourselves. It takes our minds off ourselves, bonds us to the person we're helping, and lifts our spirits. This is what Jesus meant when He said it was more blessed to give than to receive (Acts 20:35).

Arthur Gordon, in his book *A Touch of Wonder*, tells of a group of young writers who met regularly to critique each other's work. Although there was undoubtedly some notable talent among them, they chose to focus primarily on what was wrong with each other's writing. Their sessions quickly escalated into small-scale wars where they enacted a scorched-earth policy. Another group formed at the same time in response to the first group. Like that group, members shared their writings and asked for feedback. Unlike the first group though, these writers tried to be encouraging whenever possible. Over the years, the two contrasting styles led to dramatically different results. From the first group, no work of significance was produced. From the second group came several successful writers, including Marjorie Rawlings, best known for her novel, *The Yearling*.

Returning to our text, the Hebrews writer urges his audience to engage in encouragement on a "daily" basis. As noted earlier, the word here has less to do with frequency than opportunity, as is made clear by the next clause, "as long as it is called Today." In other words, we should encourage others as we have the opportunity to do so.

But it is not always easy or natural for us to encourage, is it? It calls us out of our comfort zones. It is much easier to, by default, drift into our usual conversations and interactions with the usual people. When we know someone is struggling, our first impulse is often to mind our own business—overlooking the fact that our brother or sister is our business (James 5:19–20). To overcome these things, we must have a strong sense of intentionality and realize an important truth of community—we cannot use our days well unless we're actively helping others to do the same.

Silver or Gold?

I heard a story on NPR about a man who was a sergeant in the Massachusetts Army National Guard. He served on the honor guard at military funerals, where his duty was to sound Taps. It is phrased that way because he didn't actually play the song (he didn't know how to play the bugle). Instead, he carried around a ceremonial bugle—a silver one fitted with a speaker in its bell. You pressed the "on" button, adjusted the volume, and it sounded Taps.

Of course, if you did it well enough, the undiscerning would never notice that you weren't playing the song.

It wasn't an ideal situation. The silver trumpets came into being because the demand for military funerals far exceeded the number of available buglers. The only solution that would provide the veterans with the service they deserved in the absence of qualified buglers was the silver trumpet with the speaker inside.

The sergeant had sounded Taps at a couple of hundred funerals and memorial services when a lady came up to him after a service and said it was the most beautiful rendition of the song she had ever heard. The fact that she thought he had played the music didn't sit well with him, so he decided to do something about it. He knew a man who played the bugle, and he agreed to teach him. The sergeant found an old bugle to practice with. The man instructed him on techniques and exercises to build up the muscles required to play the instrument. It took some time and effort, but eventually, he learned Taps well enough to replace the silver bugle at services with one he actually played.

But he didn't stop there. He started teaching others in the honor guard to play Taps. He's now played the song at almost 500 services. Regarding his decision to play Taps rather than sound it, he said it was "the right thing to do" and "hopefully, one day someone will do it for me." In other words, he is practicing the Golden Rule, the principle taught by Jesus in Matthew 7:12.

The sergeant is a man who is passionate about bringing encouragement to others in his own special way —to the point that unless he is doing his best for them, he isn't satisfied. That's a view of community that is as noble as it is needed. Most of us are willing to check the community box and do what we think we are expected to do, and there's something to be said about showing up with our silver bugles. But to move beyond that as the sergeant did and enter the land of the Golden Rule—that's holy ground.

Sometimes in life, in areas where we would least expect it, what really matters is the difference between silver and gold. To live well this day for Jesus means that we choose to give the best of ourselves to others as we practice "community watch."

The word becomes flesh: Most of us interact with several people during the day, receiving and giving encouragement. Try to look for that person in your path who is going through a challenging time or who maybe just needs some support and reach out to them. They will be blessed by it, and so will you.

Daily Bread

"Give us today our daily bread."
(Matthew 6:11)

My brother told me about two of his grandchildren who were playfully wrestling on the floor, with the older one seemingly getting the better of the slightly larger, younger child. He was watching and wondering if and when he should get involved. Finally, he verbally suggested the older child back off a bit. The younger one looked up at him and said, "It is okay, Granddad, I've got this covered," and immediately proceeded to reverse the situation. Hold on to this, and we'll come back to it in just a bit.

The model prayer

The petition for our daily bread is part of Jesus's prayer to His disciples in Matthew 6:9–13. I'm a huge believer in, a proponent for, and practitioner of the model prayer. I've written about it elsewhere (*Praying in the Reign*) but suffice it to say, it provides us with a wonderful (though not exhaustive) outline for kingdom prayer. My life and that of countless others down through the ages have been enriched, nurtured, and guided by these simple yet sublime words.

In some ways, the request for daily bread seems like it doesn't belong in the prayer. After all, the prayer addresses God's holiness, the coming of the kingdom, being a force for forgiveness, and fighting temptation. In that context, daily bread might seem inconsequential and mundane—but it isn't. Interestingly, it is the only element of the prayer that has "daily" attached to it.

What did Jesus mean when He told us to pray for our daily bread? Whatever else He was saying, this much is clear: with each day that stretches out before us, we're to seek God's provision for our needs—those we are aware of and those we aren't; those we think we have covered and those we are clueless about.

This means it is a prayer with an expiration date. Jesus is quite clear on the matter. He didn't say we we're to pray for tomorrow's bread or next week's but rather today's bread. That means the prayer has an expiration date of 24 hours. If we want God's provisions for tomorrow, we must take it up with Him then, not today.

How many of us practice this? If not, I suspect part of the reason for many of us is that, like my brother's younger grandchild, we believe we already have the situation under control. After all, we have plenty of food in our refrigerator and pantry, grocery stores and restaurants around us, money in our bank account (and a line of credit on our card)—"It is okay, Lord, we've got this covered." There's no need to trouble the Almighty about something we can take care of ourselves.

When we think this, an ugly little fault line of idolatry zigzags its way through our faith. It neatly compartmentalizes life into what we can do on our own and what we need God to do. We have somehow allowed ourselves to be convinced God isn't involved in absolutely everything we do and are. Despite texts like Acts 17:28, 1 Corinthians 4:7, 15:10 *et al,* we have swallowed the idea that we are self-sufficient in certain areas. God does not exist for us in them. We have become practical atheists.

The God of the Gaps

Though it is difficult to pinpoint precisely when and where the phrase came into being, the concept behind "the God of the gaps" has been around for a long time. The idea is a simple one: God is called in only to explain those matters (gaps) we don't completely understand or can't fully explain. For example, prior to the law of gravity being formulated, it was viewed by many as something God mysteriously did. With the work of Galileo, Newton, and later Einstein, gravity began to be explained in scientific terms. This knowledge bridged the "gap" in our understanding, and there was no longer a need to explain it in terms of the activity of God.

God's diminishing involvement in life and the world as our knowledge base inevitably grows is just one of the problems with this concept. The other flaw is that viewing the Almighty as a God of the gaps mistakenly assumes that because we understand how something works, we've somehow eliminated the need for God to be involved in the process.

Why is that so?

Once gravity has been explained as an attracting force between two objects affected by mass and distance, the job isn't done. There's always the more basic question to be asked, "Why is it that way?" We can only shrug our shoulders and say, "Well, that's just the nature of reality."

Fair enough, but it is the nature of reality because God made it that way! That is the truth behind the truth. Humans can explain many things but can create nothing! It is like the story about a group of scientists who thought they knew enough to challenge God to a creation contest. They were going to see who could create a superior human being. The day of the contest arrived, and the scientists showed up and started setting up their equipment. One of them took a jar and bent down to collect some dirt when God's booming voice said, "Excuse me, that's My dirt—you'll have to make your own."

Creation is God's domain; without it, there wouldn't be anything for anyone to study. The ability to understand and explain how something works doesn't justify dismissing God any more than saying a rainbow is the reflection, refraction, and dispersion of sunlight through water particles. This doesn't mean God didn't have anything to do with it (Genesis 9:13–17)! Neither truth is exclusive of the other. Viewing God as only involved in certain areas of our world or our lives is mistaken theology and makes for a confused biography.

The same thing is true regarding our daily bread—the fact that we have a role in it doesn't justify the conclusion that we no longer need God's provision. Paul says in 1 Corinthians 15:10 that he worked long and hard for Jesus, yet in the same breath, he informs us that it was "not I, but the grace of God that was with me." He tells the disciples at Philippi "to continue to work out your salvation with fear and trembling, for it is God who works in you to will and to act in order to fulfill his good purpose" (Philippians 2:12–13). There is no dichotomy between what we do versus what God does for us—it is organic.

It is the same way regarding our daily bread. Working for it doesn't preclude asking for it because we rely on God *for everything!*

God's Faithfulness

There's another important dimension involved in praying for our daily bread—reminding ourselves of God's fidelity. I was thinking about Him providing my daily bread not too long ago, and I calculated that He has been doing so for over 24,000 days. That's a long record of faithfulness. I won't pretend that I've thought to pray for it on all or even most of those days. Nonetheless, it has been there, and I'm humbled to have received God's constant care despite my inconsistent ways.

I drove by a bakery for several years on my way to work. It was not a small, mom-and-pop place but an industrial-strength, assembly-line operation that employed close to 150 people. It was large enough that when you passed by, you could smell the bread from inside your vehicle—and this was true no matter how early I went to work. The pleasant aroma told me someone had been up way ahead of me, baking the bread for today.

That's the way it is with our Father. While daily bread is often an afterthought, a small thought, or something of no thought for us, it is not that way with Him. He's been up long before us, preparing for our needs. What we receive each day is neither accidental nor incidental—it is the gift from a Father who never forgets and always provides. To posit this in our prayer life will help us grow in awareness and appreciation of God's faithfulness and daily provision for us.

A Final Word from Jeremiah

Sometime after the fall of Jerusalem in 586 B.C., the prophet Jeremiah composed the book we know as Lamentations. Jerusalem had been destroyed, and Judah was exiled because they refused to turn from their wicked ways (2 Chronicles 36:11–21). No one knew this better than Jeremiah, who had been on the front lines serving as one of God's prophets to the nation during this time (v. 12).

Because God is faithful even when His people aren't, He purged them with destruction and exile to bring them back to Him. As Jeremiah mourned over the enormity of what had happened to Israel—the atrocities related to the invasion they had experienced as well as their post-invasion trauma and suffering—he emptied his heart out.

> *My eyes fail from weeping,*
> *I am in torment within;*
> *my heart is poured out on the ground*
> *because my people are destroyed,*
> *because children and infants faint*
> *in the streets of the city.*
>
> *They say to their mothers,*
> *"Where is bread and wine?"*
> *as they faint like the wounded*
> *in the streets of the city,*
> *as their lives ebb away*
> *in their mothers' arms.*
>
> *What can I say for you?*
> *With what can I compare you,*
> *Daughter Jerusalem?*
> *To what can I liken you,*
> *that I may comfort you,*
> *Virgin Daughter Zion?*
> *Your wound is as deep as the sea.*
> *Who can heal you?*
> (Lamentations 2:11–13)

Then in about the middle of the book, he penned these remarkable words:

> *Yet I call this to mind and therefore I have hope:*
> *Because of the Lord's great love we are not consumed*
> *For His compassions never fail.*
> *They are new every morning;*
> *great is your faithfulness.*

I say to myself, "The LORD is my portion;
therefore I will wait for him." (Lamentations 3:21–24)

Despite everything that had occurred, Jeremiah found hope by anchoring in God's character. Although Israel had brought terrible judgment on themselves through their persistent waywardness, God had not given up on them. He would heal their wounds, restore the nation, and send the Messiah to them.

Although more than twenty-five centuries have passed since those words were written, Jeremiah's words should frame our approach to life today. The Lord is our portion, and His compassions are new every morning. In prosperity, adversity, and everything in between—we will look to Him to provide!

The word becomes flesh: Again, including the principles of the model prayer in our prayers will make us aware of our dependency upon God. Speaking of prayer, many young children go through a stage when they thank God for *everything*. They soon outgrow this but hearing such a prayer (and being around young dependents) reminds us of both our dependency and our call to be like children before God.

Not By Bread Alone

Now the Berean Jews were of more noble character than those in Thessalonica,
for they received the message with great eagerness and examined
the Scriptures every day to see if what Paul said was true.
(Acts 17:11)

Relationships fall apart when there is no communication.

W hen we hear a statement like that, many of us think about people who are married or perhaps on their way to getting married. Of course, this can also apply to friendships, families, relationships at work, or in whatever form they exist. It certainly applies to our relationship with God.

If we want a relationship with God based on truth rather than emotions, tradition, culture, or anything else, then we will root it in His word. Along with prayer, it is a primary component in communicating with our Father. In regard to His word, we are to possess an attitude that eagerly searches, lovingly listens and promptly responds (1 Samuel 3:1–10).

Inside the Synagogue

In our text, Paul and Silas followed their well-established custom of going to the synagogue when they entered a city and speaking to the people there. A few chapters earlier, in Acts 13, Luke gives us the content of one of those messages. It was addressed to the people in the synagogue at Antioch. If you read the message (vv. 16–41), it is clear what was going on—Paul and Silas were using *words* to appeal to them. They weren't just any words—they were quotes from the Old Testament or about the history recorded there. These spokesmen for God also used words of their own that He had given them through the Spirit to reach out to the people with the message of Jesus (John 16:12–15).

There wasn't anything magical or mystical going on—although God was definitely involved (Acts 16:13–14). They didn't have the people close their eyes, ask the Holy Spirit in, or turn down the lights while soft music played. They called on them to accept and act on their words concerning Christ. That was the issue. They didn't think there was anything unspiritual or legalistic about it. No one accused them of bibliolatry. This was simply what God wanted them to do everywhere they went (Matthew 28:18–20).

Beginning in Jerusalem

We see the same kind of thing in Acts 2 when the church had its beginning. There, we're told:

> With many other words he warned them; and he pleaded with them, "Save yourselves from this corrupt generation." Those who accepted his message were baptized, and about three thousand were added to their number that day. (vv. 41–42)

People came into a relationship with God when they accepted Peter's message concerning Jesus by repenting and being baptized (v. 38). Make no mistake about it—they were reconciled to God through the atoning work of Jesus, but it was communicated through words (see 1 Corinthians 2:13ff.).

The communities of faith that came into being because of people responding to the message of God continued to be nurtured, sustained, and guided by words. That wasn't the only thing, but it was fundamental. (There's a reason the Scripture speaks of God's word as being milk, meat, honey, nourishment, etc.). Read any of the letters to the churches, and you'll see this borne out. They develop essential spiritual principles and truths and contain important instructions about how Christian are to live their lives. The early disciples didn't look for their cues from social media, celebrities, or the government— they listened to God as He spoke through the apostles and prophets.

While we have no apostles or prophets today, God continues to speak to us from Scripture as He spoke to Israel in ancient times. The Scriptures the Bereans were searching in our text probably refers to the Old Testament (but see 1 Timothy 5:18; Luke 10:7). They were taking the message of Paul and Silas and seeing if it lined up with what was taught there. Luke tells us that this was a *noble* characteristic. It showed they were serious enough about their relationship with God to research Paul and Silas's claims concerning Jesus and His kingdom. Access to Scripture was much more limited during their time since it was all hand-copied, so there's a good possibility they were coming together at the synagogue to do this rather than pursuing it individually. As a result of this, we're told "many of them believed" (17:12).

The Example of Jesus

When Satan confronted Jesus in the wilderness, he tempted Him to turn the stones into bread to ease His famished condition. Christ replied that "Man shall not live on bread alone, but on every word that comes from the mouth of God" (Matthew 4:4). He was saying something with those words! A man in the wilderness with nothing to eat for almost six weeks is worth paying attention to, and He only wished to speak about being sustained by God's word.

He was saying (among other things) that we cannot survive on a diet of Instagram, Netflix, ESPN, or any other unceasing entertainment options available to us. We must have food from our Father! This is what Israel was meant to learn from their wilderness experience but didn't (Deuteronomy 8:2–3).

But He was saying something even more. What Satan really wanted to control wasn't Jesus' diet—he wanted to control Him. He wanted Jesus to use His power in selfish ways rather than as a servant of God. Turning the stones into bread would have been the first step on such an agenda, but Christ rejected this narrative. His ministry and His life would continue to reflect His dependency on God and be shaped by His word. Our challenge is the same. The world would have us frame our lives in terms of its kingdom. The narrative would involve things like self-fulfillment, social status, involvement in the latest social or political cause, and whatever else is trending. As disciples, we're part of Jesus' kingdom. That means the narrative we follow is to walk in His steps and live by the words of God. That's our story and we're sticking to it!

Living Under the Influence

The letters to the Ephesians and the Colossians were written by the same person (Paul) at the same time (during his first imprisonment) and were delivered by the same person (Tychicus). Both churches were in Asia, and although they certainly had differences, they also possessed many similarities. Given this, it is not surprising that we find many parallel passages in the two letters. Sections in both letters deal with households (Ephesians 5:21—6:9; Colossians 3:18—4:1), the old and new nature (Ephesians 4:22–32; Colossians 3:5–12), and what we're interested in—living under the Spirit's influence (Ephesians 5:18-20; Colossians 3:15-17).

In the Ephesians text, Paul writes, "Be filled with the Spirit" (5:19), while in Colossians, it is, "Let the word of Christ dwell in you richly" (3:16, ESV). He's not equating the Spirit with the word (or "the message," as other translations render it) any more than we should equate these two letters. What he is doing is employing a metonymy—substituting the cause (the Spirit) for the effect (the word) since it is the Spirit who is associated with the giving of the word/message of Jesus (John 16:12–15; 2 Peter 1:19–21). Therefore, "filled with the Spirit" in Ephesians is "Let the word of Christ dwell in you richly" in Colossians. Someone who is under the influence of the Spirit has the word of Christ dwelling in them richly. They are living by the word of God.

Where Do I Start?
How Do I Get More Out of the Bible?

These two questions represent the struggles of a substantial number of people concerning God's word. To some extent, they are related. If you don't get off to a good start and benefit from what you are reading, you will probably find it difficult to spend time consistently in God's word. Therefore, it is important to find a good place to start.

Where is that place? The answer might surprise you. You can begin in just about any place that interests you. From my point of view, the more critical component is *how* you start. Many people have difficulty getting traction in

God's word because they read it cafeteria-style—a few verses here and a few there. Few books are meant to be read that way, and that is true of the Bible. It is a collection of books, and the best way to maximize your understanding of it is to read it the way it was written—book by book.

One of the benefits of reading a book of the Bible, as opposed to random verses, is that it is much easier to keep up with the context. Each book was written to a specific group of people for a specific purpose (or often several of them). For example, if you decide to read Paul's letter to the Philippians, then with just a little digging, you can find sufficient background information to provide you with the framework for understanding the letter. Once you have an idea of what was being said to the original audience and why, you can take the next step and ask what it is saying to you. But it all begins with learning to be a book inspector rather than a verse collector.

In addition to what your church offers through its classes and assemblies, being part of a Bible study group can also be quite beneficial in helping you get more out of God's word. Studying the Scripture in community enables us to look at the text through several sets of eyes. This almost always results in more insights and applications than we would think of on our own. However, group study is not without some potential pitfalls. One is that we can allow it to replace, rather than supplement, our personal time in the word. Another is that sometimes groups (usually those lacking experienced leadership) can fall into situations where they end up pooling their ignorance more than searching the Scriptures. Avoid these hazards, and group study can be a great blessing.

The Voice of Our Father

The soldier was deployed overseas when his son was just three months old. Before that, he had put him to bed every evening, so after he left, the infant had trouble going to sleep at night. His mother decided to get a "daddy doll"—a specially made figurine with her husband's picture on it. After that, the baby went to bed with the "daddy doll" every night and fell asleep without any trouble. The doll even had a chip inside with a recording of his father speaking comforting words. Whenever her son was upset, his mother activated the voice feature, and it immediately calmed him down.

The voice of your father will do that.

In our Bibles, we're blessed with the unmistakable voice of our Father. We don't have to live at the mercy of our impulses. We don't have to wonder about questions of basic morality. We're told who we are, where we came from, where we're going, and why we're here. We don't have to be driven by our culture's trends, fashions, and flavors as though there is nothing more transcendent than whatever a given people have chosen to make popular in a given place and time. Thank God for that!

Biblical truth is "God making His presence known and felt" (McGuiggan). The voice of our Father comforts us when we are distraught, and it teaches us how to live, love, and find true joy in our lives. It tells of God's relentless and redeeming love, Jesus' glorious life, and the hope that flows from it. It provides us with inspiring examples of men and women who have lived with courage and character in the face of overwhelming adversity.

God doesn't call us all to be Bible scholars or exegetes of Scripture, but He does call us to read, think, and submit. We're not to pursue the biblical witness as an end in itself or as though knowing about God is our goal—we put His word in our hearts so we might know Him through Jesus (John 5:39–40, 17:3).

Now I commit you to God and to the word of his grace, which can build you up and give you an inheritance among all those who are sanctified.
(Acts 20:32).

The word becoming flesh: Thanks to technology, we are blessed to have God's word available to us in innumerable ways. Many enjoy listening to God's word, while others might journal their way through it. Perhaps the most important thing is not the medium but the consistency that comes when you establish a regular time and place to listen to God as He speaks through His word. If you don't have some kind of established habit, why not start one today? The benefits are out of this world!

Wear It or Bear It?

*"Whoever wants to be my disciple must deny themselves and
take up their cross daily and follow me."*
(Luke 9:23)

What do you think—are there more people wearing the cross or bearing the cross? The cross has always been a popular design for jewelry. Some wear it without thought, while others attach deep significance to their cross-wearing: it will protect them, it is a sign they belong to Jesus, or it is simply their way of acknowledging God. While Christ never asked anyone to wear a cross, He is quite interested in us taking up our cross and following Him.

The Gospel of Luke

Luke addressed his gospel as well as the book of Acts to "most excellent Theophilus" (Luke 1:3). There are all sorts of ideas about who Theophilus was—from Paul's lawyer, to a high priest, to simply someone who loved God ("Theophilus" literally means "lover/friend of God"). Since the phrase "most excellent" is used elsewhere in reference to Roman officials (Acts 23:26 (NASB), 24:3, 26:25), it seems likely that Theophilus was a Roman official who was a disciple of Jesus. With the books of Luke and Acts, Luke was furnishing him with a thorough account of Jesus and the church so that he might "know the certainty of the things" he had been taught (Luke 1:4).

Discipleship texts are an important element of Luke's gospel. The most extensive one is 14:25–35, where Jesus tells His followers that unless they are willing for Him to be Lord of their relationships, their possessions, and their lives, they "cannot be My disciple" (v. 26, 33, 27). Another text is 9:57–63, where Jesus encounters three people who all desire to follow Him. His reply to each of them stresses the radical nature of what it means to be a disciple of Jesus.

Then there is our text in 9:23. What Jesus says here is in some ways more expansive than 14:27 ("Whoever does not carry their cross and follow me cannot be my disciple"). Two additional elements are mentioned in 9:23— denying self and *daily* carrying our cross. Both of these are important. The mention of self-denial helps define precisely what Jesus had in mind by His use of the cross metaphor. At the same time, the word "daily" alerts us to the truth that carrying our cross isn't a one-and-done act by disciples (like baptism)—it's something that needs to be realized on a regular basis. Beyond these two elements, what is the overarching message of the verse, and how should it shape our efforts to live within each day for God?

Up Close and Personal

It is helpful to note that this call for discipleship occurs in a section David Tiede (*Luke*) characterizes as *revealing*. In the verses preceding it, Peter has identified Jesus as "God's Messiah" (v. 20). This truth had been revealed to him by God (Matthew 16:17) and contrasted with what the crowds thought about Him (Luke 9:18–19). There is a second revealing in v. 22 as Jesus shared with His disciples the true meaning of being the Messiah—"The Son of Man must suffer many things and be rejected by the elders, the chief priests and the teachers of the law, and he must be killed and on the third day be raised to life."

Of course, this revealing was much more difficult for the disciples to accept, and a third revealing reinforced it—Jesus' transfiguration—where He appeared in "glorious splendor" as He spoke with Moses and Elijah about His "departure, which He was about to bring to fulfillment at Jerusalem" (v. 31). These revealings are critical to Luke's narrative, as they strip away popular misconceptions about the Christ and point us to His mission of redemption.

In the midst of these revealings is the one we are concerned with (v. 23). It has to do with what it means to be a disciple of Jesus. As the cross is fundamental to Jesus' identity, it is also central to those who follow Him. The cross speaks of death, to be sure, but we must be judicious. While Jesus' death on the cross was unquestionably the ultimate act of love and submission to God, we must not isolate it from the rest of His life. What happened at the cross was the outworking of a lifetime of joyful, daily surrender. In that sense, Jesus was always carrying the cross.

The Cross and Joy

This provides the context for us as we think about what it means to carry our cross for Jesus each day. It involves the same joyful submission to God's will, as opposed to following our own will. You'll notice I've mentioned joy in reference to Jesus and us. That's because brokenness and joy go together. Unconditional surrender leads to unqualified joy. There is no other way.

When David sought God's forgiveness after his adultery with Bathsheba and murder of Uriah, he spoke of having "a broken spirit" and "a broken and contrite heart" (Psalm 51:17). (The only people who are whole are those whose lives are broken to self and open to God.) But notice that he also asked that God would, "Let me hear joy and gladness; let the bones You have crushed rejoice" (v. 7). He wanted a pure heart (v. 10) and the joy that went with it (v. 12).

Jesus did not sin, yet He knew better than anyone the brokenness to self that carrying the cross represented, and because of it (not in spite of it), He was a person of great joy (John 15:11, 17:13). He was invited to weddings, children flocked to Him, and He was the opposite of the decidedly unjoyful Pharisees. It is ironic that some believers avoid taking up their cross because they think it will mean missing out on life when it is precisely the means by which we truly experience life!

The Cross and Grace

How do we live out the brokenness the cross calls us to on a daily basis? The answer is … we can't do it on our own. We must have God's empowering grace. That's why Paul told the disciples at Philippi to "work out your salvation with fear and trembling, for it is God who works in you to will and to act in order to fulfill His good purposes." (See something similar in 1 Corinthians 15:10.) We work outward because God works within. We can't live out the beautiful life of brokenness on our own, but we can with God's help.

The Only Way

The call to take up our cross daily is unequivocal, and we must not compromise it to appease ourselves or others. Trying to live as a follower of Jesus without carrying our cross is like trying to drive a car by putting it in neutral, sticking one leg out the door, and pushing off with our foot. That's not the way a vehicle is designed to work, and attempting to "drive" in this manner will exhaust us and get us nowhere. C.S. Lewis addressed this In *Mere Christianity* when he wrote:

> The terrible thing, the almost impossible thing, is to hand over your whole self—all your wishes and precautions—to Christ. But it is far easier than what we are all trying to do instead. For what we are trying to do is to remain what we call "ourselves," to keep personal happiness as our great aim in life, and yet at the same time be "good."

> We are all trying to let our mind and heart go their own way-centered on money or pleasure or ambition—and hoping, in spite of this, to behave honestly and chastely and humbly. And that is exactly what Christ warned us you could not do.

If your life isn't broken, then you haven't allowed God to fix it! Over a century ago, Jessie Browns Pound wrote a song called, *The Way of the Cross Leads Home.* Here is the song's first verse:

> I must needs go home by the way of the cross,
> There's no other way but this;
> I shall ne'er get sight of the gates of light.
> If the way of the cross I miss.

There is a myriad of ways that are currently promised, promoted, and pointed to in our culture as leading us home. I suppose it has always been that way. Many of them look good and sound appealing. They offer us prosperity, popularity, self-fulfillment, and whatever else that is trending. But they all have one thing in common—none of them lead home! In this era of over-inclusiveness and over-indulgence, it is critical that we understand there is only one way that leads home—the way of the cross. It is the only way home because it was the way of Jesus, and we will never go wrong following Him.

We must not hesitate to include cross-bearing in our message for people in the process of coming to the Lord. Not only because it belongs there (it is part of the biblical concept of repentance) but also because we shouldn't underestimate the God-given hunger people can have for giving themselves completely to something, or to be more precise, Someone. Brooks notes that:

> What most people want in life, especially when young, is not happiness, but an intensity that reaches to the core. We want to be involved in some important pursuit that involves hardship and is worthy of that hardship . . . there is something inside us that longs for some calling that requires dedication and sacrifice.

Back to our text in Luke 9, Jesus made it clear in v. 24 that by "losing" our life in this way, we will find it. This is the paradox that faith calls us to—to trust that in letting go of our old life, God will provide us with a glorious new one.

This is what the disciples of Jesus needed to see and what the transfiguration so powerfully revealed. They thought there was nothing glorious about Jesus' dying, but they couldn't have been more mistaken. The cross was glorious because it revealed Christ and God. It was glorious because it became the means for the redemption of humanity. It was glorious because it fulfilled the Scripture. And all that was pictured as the glorified Jesus spoke with Elijah and Moses about His "departure." No wonder it took place on top of a mountain!

This is precisely how we are to get on with carrying our cross. What we once thought of as having little or no glory we come to recognize as being more glorious than we ever imagined. It's that way because it is the way of the Lord of Glory. It is that way because it is the way of His glorious kingdom— where we find peace, joy, and purpose. It is glorious because it is the way of community—we find true fellowship as a cross-bearing people.

Checked Your Hands Lately?

Living under the lordship of Jesus means we live each day with open hands rather than clenched fists. We recognize that whatever God has blessed us with physically, relationally, materially—it all belongs to Him, and we trust His reign over those things (Luke 14:33). To live this way is to live with a pure (single) heart that seeks God's kingdom above all (Matthew 5:8, 6:33). To live this way is to live as salt, and it is "good" for us and the world (Luke 14:34).

To live with open hands means we don't become too comfortable or overly attached to present and pleasant realities. There is a profound blessing in recognizing our transience (Psalm 39:4) and journeying by faith (84:5).

The Terminal is a movie about a man named Victor Navorski. He is from the fictional country of Krakozhia and has traveled to America. He deplanes at Kennedy International in New York only to find out the government of Krakozhia has collapsed, and his passport is no longer valid. He cannot enter the United States, nor can he leave it—he is trapped at the airport. The bulk of the movie shows us how Navorski adjusts to his new life and the challenges of living at the airport.

In many ways, living at the airport is a fitting metaphor for disciples of Jesus. Earth is our airport. We came in on one flight, and before you know it, we'll be leaving on another. It is okay to enjoy the airport, but we don't want to get too attached to it. If we spend too much time in the gift shop, it can weigh us down or even cause us to miss our flight. We must remember that our citizenship is in heaven (Philippians 3:20–21). Our mission while at the airport is to bring heaven to earth. This can only be done by people who live with a continued consciousness of the cross.

The word becomes flesh: For some, wearing the cross might be just the visual cue they need to make them mindful of Jesus' call to carry our cross. For others, including "Your kingdom come, Your will to be done, on earth as it is in heaven," in their prayers is helpful. For all disciples, the Supper each week should call us to remember the One who "died for all, that those who live should no longer live for themselves but for him who died for them and was raised again" (2 Corinthians 5:15).

Blessed Are the Grinders

As long as it is day, we must do the works of him who sent me.
Night is coming, when no one can work.
(John 9:4)

Her name was Virginia. She had been diagnosed with an aggressive brain tumor. I remember during one of our visits, she told me she was "just trying to take things one day at a time." She passed away not long after that. That was more than 30 years ago, and every time I've heard that statement since then, it has always been in the context of someone dealing with a major crisis of some sort. I've never heard anyone say, "We're going to continue to take things one day at a time." I'm probably being too literal here, but if our words mean things, why do we wait until a full-blown trauma before we start to live life the way God intended?

Almost as disturbing is the disconnect that exists between daily living and work. By *work,* I mean primarily what we do to earn a living but also activities that call for a commitment of our time, energy, or presence. Have you noticed when you hear or read what others have to say about learning to live one day at a time how very little tends to be said concerning work? I recently finished such a book (over 200 pages) that made scant mention of the subject. For whatever reason, work and making the most of a day don't seem to be regarded complementary subjects. That's a shame since work occupies such a significant place in our lives. Any approach to living that doesn't embrace it is seriously lacking.

Jesus spoke of work when He told His disciples: "As long as it is day, we must do the works of Him who sent me. Night is coming, when no one can work. While I am in the world, I am the light of the world" (John 9:4–5). Christ had a sense of urgency regarding His work. He understood He had a limited amount of time to accomplish His mission. As a result, He was focused and worked to impart that urgency to His disciples.

Of course, Jesus' task was a redemptive one—the salvation of the world through His death on the cross. As part of that mission, He trained the 12 apostles and ministered to the world around Him. Because of this, I suppose we might be tempted to dismiss this text as irrelevant to our lives.

But we would be wrong in doing so.

God created us to work. Before the curse, Adam was placed in the garden "to work it and take care of it" (Genesis 2:15). As his helper (v. 18), there's no reason to believe that Eve didn't join in after she came on the scene. Several important points flow from this: 1) work was part of a perfect world, 2) it is part of how we image God (Exodus 20:8–11), and 3) it should be much more than just a means to an end (i.e., earning a living).

After establishing the grace-based nature of our relationship with God (Ephesians 2:8–9), Paul goes on to tell us we have been "created in Christ to do good works, which God prepared in advance for us to do" (v. 10). This would certainly include what we do on our jobs (see 4:28). Paul mentions work in 1 Thessalonians 4:11–12 as an important component of a "daily life" that will help us to "win the respect of outsiders." After all, work is one of the fundamental ways we make ourselves useful to others and contribute to the world around us. In his book *Every Good Endeavor,* Timothy Keller says, "There may be no better way to love your neighbor than to simply do your work. But only skillful, competent work will do."

Work is a blessing because when we engage in it for the right reasons, it answers to our nature and calling. Is there a better feeling than that of a job well done? Correspondingly, to have the ability to work and not do so robs us of an important component of our God-given identity. When we don't work, we miss out on the purpose and dignity that flows from it. Take that away, and you've removed something fundamental from the fabric of any culture.

The Daily Grind

We don't always view work as a blessing, though, do we? Part of the reason for this is that for all of us, there are routine, monotonous aspects to whatever type of work we do. Add to that the fact that we don't always experience the results we would like to from the efforts we put forth.

Furthermore, work usually involves the prime hours of our day. Put it all together, and we're devoting the prime time of our day to routine, monotonous activities that sometimes don't seem to accomplish much—and that's how we can end up viewing our work as "the daily grind."

In response to that, it is easy for us to dream of doing something else—something where there is a closer, more tangible connection between our efforts and results. While there can be noble aspects to such a vision, it is also healthy to ask ourselves, "Does my desire to do something else go beyond simply wanting to fulfill my personal sense of accomplishment?" If the answer is "no," then what you're really pursuing probably isn't ministry as much as having a good feeling at the end of the day. Maybe your real challenge isn't finding something more gratifying but changing your attitude about what you're doing now. I'm not suggesting this is true for everyone (if God is calling you to something else, then get busy with it!), but I think it is worth considering for anyone who is struggling with their daily grind and dreams of something better.

Teresa of Calcutta may or may not have been the first to say, "We can do no great things, just small things with great love." But whoever originally said it, I'd like to think they had in mind the grinders of the world—the people who get up every day and give the prime time of their day (and their lives) to working in some *seemingly* insignificant way. But is it truly insignificant? Do they have the opportunity to touch the lives of other people? Are they producing a product or a service that is helpful to others?

Was Moses involved in insignificant work while herding sheep for his father-in-law? It wouldn't have charted with anyone, but he was doing exactly what God wanted him to do. What about Paul making tents or Jesus working in Joseph's trade of carpentry (or was it building, as some suggest)? Don't forget Lydia and her purple cloth or the centurion Cornelius. We'd all like to be involved in work that will win us a Nobel Prize, but there are only so many of those to go around. The rest of us must learn to find contentment in giving ourselves to "the ordinary." Qualify that any way you need to, but don't overlook the fact that God must love the ordinary since He made so much of it and uses it all the time.

Any work that is honorable and done well is pleasing to Him. For many of us, rather than pining away and dreaming of doing something else, we would be far better off figuring out how to make a difference for God in what we're currently doing. I'm not sure that in the end, the work of the kingdom isn't so much *what* we do but *how* we do it (1 Corinthians 13:1–3). Despite its grind, work is a blessing and a meaningful way we bring blessings to others.

Working with Light

Returning to our text in John 9, it occurs in a section where there is a cluster of light both in words and images. *Light* is an important term for John as it occurs 25 times in his gospel. He employs it seven times when speaking of Jesus in 1:4–9. There are similar clusters in 3:19–21 and 12:35–46. Then, there is the section where our text is located. "Light" is used three times here, and the imagery of light is a key part of the overall context.

It begins in chapter 7, where we're told of Jesus' presence at the Feast of the Tabernacles in Jerusalem. The Israelites celebrated this feast by constructing and living in temporary structures for seven days to remind them of the 40 years their ancestors lived in tents in the wilderness (Leviticus 23:42–43). In addition, the Levites built giant menorahs that were placed in the temple courtyard to illuminate the evening sky. This spoke to them of God's presence (*Shekinah*) in the pillar of fire during those wilderness years (Exodus 40:36–38). What a sight it must have been to hear the roar, feel the heat, and watch as the enormous flames danced skyward, illuminating the temple area. It is in this context that Jesus claimed He was not only the light of the Jewish nation—but of the world (8:12).

John also tells us about Jesus' meeting with a man who was blind (9:1). His entire life he had known only darkness. When Christ opened the man's eyes, he went from night to light. By bringing him to this state, God's works (His mercy, power, and goodness) were being displayed (v. 3).

Jesus goes on to say this is why we are here. While it is light (day), it is our mission to "work the works" of God (v. 4, ESV). There will come a time when we won't be able to do this, but while we can, we are to be involved in activities that display and manifest God's nature. With this text (and others), we learn that work is more than something to do—it is an avenue through which God's goodness is revealed.

There are spiritual overtones to any work that is done well and to the glory of the Father. Does anyone seriously think Adam and Eve were just doing "busy work" when they cultivated the garden? They were partnering with God in displaying His love. Do we honestly think we're merely "supporting our families" or communities through the paid or unpaid tasks that we do? We are displaying God's character. Look at Paul's letter to Titus and note how many times he mentions "good" in reference to what they do, teach, or love. (I counted eight). Think about God looking upon His creative work and seeing it was *good*. We need to see the connection between who we are and what we do!

I suppose it is human nature to gauge our work as significant or insignificant. We tend to be enamored with anything associated with *making a difference*. While that's not all bad, it is not all good either because we often don't see the whole picture, do we? This mindset also overlooks the truth that significant accomplishments often occur due to small, incremental actions that take place over great lengths of time. There's nothing that makes a greater difference in the world than raising a child, but any parent with grown children can tell you there is a sowing season and a reaping season— and there is often quite a bit of time between the two.

Learning from Loaves and Fishes

We're all familiar with the story of the boy who shared his loaves and fishes with Jesus. What did Christ do with them? Amazing things! What can He do with our loaves and fishes? *Whatever needs to be done!* This is where it gets a bit tricky because we would all like to see our loaves and fishes feed multitudes. We'd like to see our work result in something spectacular or at least substantial. But that's not for us to say. In that sense, we're in supply rather than distribution. We sow, and we water, but it is God who gives the increase—and we must trust Him to do so.

Let me conclude with four ways to implement what has been discussed in this section.

1. **Invite God into your work.** He's already there, of course, but He longs to be involved at the deepest level and is waiting to be asked.
2. **Offer your work to God.** In his nurturing book of prayers, *Every Moment Holy* (Vol. 1), Douglas McKelvey has this at the conclusion of a liturgy for one who is an employee:
   And may the outworking of the gospel be always evident in my work, that my service as an employee might be ever reckoned and received as first rendered unto you, O Christ.
3. **View your work as a way of making God known.** All work touches people, sooner or later, in some way. We are to understand and view our work as an opportunity to bring to light the work and goodness of God, so how we do our work is just as important as the final product.
4. **Remember God is sovereign over your work.** We need to trust God to use our work in whatever way is best for His kingdom and glory.

Mary Ann Evans, who wrote under the name George Eliot, ends her novel *Middlemarch* with a powerful observation concerning the novel's heroine, Dorothea. Dorothea seemed destined for great things yet ends up living a conventional life as a wife and mother. Eliot offers these words of explanation for her very ordinary life:

> But the effect of her being on those around her was incalculably diffusive: for the growing good of the world is partly dependent on unhistoric acts; and that things are not so ill with you and me as they might have been is half owing to the number who lived faithfully a hidden life, and rest in unvisited tombs.

The word becoming flesh: "Whatever you do, work at it with all your heart, as working for the Lord, not for human masters, since you know that you will receive an inheritance from the Lord as a reward. It is the Lord Christ you are serving" (Colossians 3:23–24). Although Paul's words were originally addressed to people living under old-world slavery, the principles of working with all your heart, offering it to the Lord, and knowing God will bless us are transcendent truths for all time. This is an excellent passage to put on our hearts!

Get Yourself Renewed

"Therefore we do not lose heart. Though outwardly are wasting away,
inwardly we are being renewed day by day."
(2 Corinthians 4:16)

Any way you care to look at it, Corinth was Paul's most challenging church. We have more writing from him to this congregation than any other (by quite a bit)—and we know of at least two more letters he wrote that haven't been preserved for us (1 Corinthians 5:9; 2:2:1–4).

Paul had his back against the wall when he wrote 2 Corinthians. His already rocky relationship with the church had further deteriorated. Several there found fault with him for multiple reasons. A few of these were:

o He was unimpressive in appearance and not a good speaker
  (2 Corinthians 10:1, 10, 11:6)
o He was fickle and undependable (1:17)
o He didn't compare favorably with the self-proclaimed apostles the
  Corinthians knew (11:5,12:11)

The last item drives much of what Paul says in 2 Corinthians 4. The "super-apostles" some at Corinth were so impressed with flaunted their self-appointed authority and power (11:18–20). They knew nothing of weakness, humility, or suffering—they were above all that. They were a first-century version of the prosperity gospel. Consequently, Paul's troubles and hardships were viewed as evidence that he was an inferior apostle—if he was one at all!

Paul's Response and Surprising Perspective

Paul defended himself against this line of reasoning by asserting the opposite—his suffering (as part of the body of Christ) was precisely what it meant to be an apostle (4:7–12)! Furthermore, the difficulties he faced didn't discourage him as some might have supposed. God's work through his adversity and affliction kept him from losing heart over his diminishing outward state (v. 16). This was why he refused to fixate on external appearances as others did, but stayed focused on deeper, unseen, eternal realities (v. 18).

At this point, it is helpful to probe deeper into the words *outwardly* and *inwardly*. What did Paul mean by them? Murray Harris (*2 Corinthians in The Expositor's Bible Commentary*) has this helpful observation:

> Paul is not thinking of two distinct entities, "the body" and "the soul" . . . but is considering his total existence from two different viewpoints. His "outer-self" is his whole person in his "creaturely mortality" . . . the physical aspect of his person; his "inner self" is his whole person as a "new creation" (5:17), the spiritual aspect of the believer.

Even though his physical body was wasting away because of his hardships, Paul found peace and renewal in knowing that through God's power, his difficulties and trials were working for him to "achieve an eternal glory" (v. 17). This "glory" extended to his body (through the resurrection) so that the life he was slowly losing would one day be restored.

Think of it like putting ice cubes in a glass of water. Although the cubes will diminish in size over time, the water that composes them doesn't disappear—it simply changes in form from solid to liquid. As the ice cubes melt, the liquid volume of water in the glass increases so that if you wanted to, you could refreeze that increase and be back where you started. In the same way, the life that is seemingly melting away in our bodies will one day be restored.

But Paul is saying something more. Our bodies will not only find life again—it will be a profoundly greater existence than what we experience now (2 Corinthians 5:1–5). Therefore, no matter what might be happening in our lives at the present time, God has given us the profound hope of a glorious future life (Romans 8:18). This is why, rather than losing heart, we can experience daily renewal.

Focused on the Flesh

This is a powerful message, and one disciples need to take to heart. We live in a culture that doesn't deal particularly well with growing old. Youth is worshiped, and consequently, we have an aversion to aging that pushes well past healthy boundaries. Any perceived diminishment of physical features is fought tooth and nail by many through surgeries, peels, liposuction, laser treatments, tucks, lifts, augmentations, reshaping, and whatever else might be available. Americans spend over $16 billion a year on cosmetic surgery. While some of that is for procedures made necessary by accident or disease, the bulk of it has to do with treatments done in an attempt to make us look younger—all so we can proclaim that "50 is the new 30."

Wanting to look the best we can is normal and healthy. Wanting to look significantly younger than we are is vanity (to say nothing of unrealistic). While there is a glory to youth, it soon fades and doesn't return. It's meant to be replaced by the glory of experience, wisdom, and age (Proverbs 16:31, 20:29). This is exactly what takes place and is celebrated in many cultures. This sometimes happens in our culture; it just doesn't get much attention. Instead, people are persuaded by advertisers, celebrities, and much of social media to spend enormous amounts of time and money pursuing the transformation of their bodies. Few sadly give any substantive thought to being renewed inwardly. Fixing their eyes through the latest procedure makes perfect sense, while fixing their eyes on what is unseen sounds strange and confusing.

Renewal Through Seeing the Unseen

If we back up a bit to 2 Corinthians 3:18, Paul says something else that is equally intriguing when he speaks of how disciples with "unveiled faces contemplate the Lord's glory are being transformed into His image with ever-increasing glory" (v. 18).

It is difficult not to look for a connection between "being renewed day by day" and "being transformed into His image." Both statements speak of continual change taking place in the lives of followers of Jesus. Both statements are in the passive voice, meaning God is the one who is ultimately doing the renewing/transforming. Both texts make it clear that important things are taking place as we submit our lives to God. These are not changes we can necessarily track with our physical vision, but they nonetheless constitute an important spiritual reality.

This also provides us with some insight about how we can make renewal and transformation greater realities in our lives. We need to think about the way we see things and whether we are leaving room to see "what is unseen" (4:18). Unseen is not unreal (think of the layers of the earth underneath our feet or all the plant and animal life below the oceans' surface). In fact, our lives abound with all sorts of unseen realities. We talk, sing about, and celebrate the unseen ideal of love. Everyone exercises faith in some manner—from trusting that the light for opposing traffic is red when yours is green to having faith in your friends and family. This ability to see the unseen is a uniquely human trait. It is a characteristic of our Father, who "calls into being things that were not" (Romans 4:17), and it is part of imaging Him.

"What is unseen" can be many things, but most of all, it is Jesus. And as we "contemplate the Lord's glory, "we are transformed into His image. While it is certainly healthy to think and speak of faith, hope, love, heaven, and everything else, in the end, it all comes back to Jesus because they are all anchored in Him. Peter tells the exiles he writes:

> Though you have not seen him, you love him; and even though you do not see him now, you believe in him and are filled with an inexpressible and glorious joy,for you are receiving the end result of your faith, the salvation of your souls. (1 Peter 1:8–9)

It is that word "inexpressible" that grabs my attention. As someone who dabbles in words, I'm generally not a big fan of such expressions because it is a writer's business to choose the word that accurately conveys the idea they want to communicate—not to lazily say it can't be described. (After all, it is not like we don't have plenty of words to choose from). Of course, there are times when you have to resort to saying something is unable to be put into words, but it seems to me that's done too frequently (very much like how the word "awesome" is used to speak of so many non-awesome things).

Checking the translations, "inexpressible" is the word of choice (NIV, ESV), followed by "unspeakable" (ASV, KJV), "indescribable" (*International Standard Version*), "no words can tell" (CEV), "which words cannot express" (*Good News Translation*) and "which cannot be spoken" (*Aramaic Bible in Plain English*). When the lexical work is done, we are back to where we started. Peter was writing under the oversight of the Spirit (John 14:25–26; 2 Peter 1:19–21). And if the Spirit guided him to choose the word best translated as "inexpressible," then that's the word that belongs here! He's telling us that the disciples he wrote to, who were experiencing "all kinds of trials" (v. 6), nonetheless possessed a joy that words were unable to describe! As we see the glory of our unseen Lord, God brings this daily transformation and renewal. We're not the same people we started out as. Each day, God is shaping us into the image of His Son and providing us with the bright hope of a certain future.

The word becoming flesh: Transformation and renewal are all around us *if* we are paying attention. Our lawns, gardens, trees, and seasons are in a constant state of transformation and renewal. These are seen realities that mirror the unseen truth of what God is doing (and will do) in our lives and should enable us to model before the world a peaceful and joyful response to aging and infirmity as we move closer to being with Him.

Living in the Now

"I tell you, now is the time of God's favor, now is the day of salvation."
(2 Corinthians 6:2)

A reminder from Rome

We can and do accomplish meaningful things each day. We all have routines we engage in to meet the daily needs and requirements of ourselves and others. Students attend class, do assignments, and take exams. Employees complete tasks associated with their job. Retirees might participate in volunteer work, play pickle ball, or visit with friends and family. But no matter who we are or how much energy and initiative we possess, the fact is many things simply can't be accomplished in a single day. Any attempt to override this truth will only lead to a fast flame-out on our part. We're all familiar with the adage, *Rome wasn't built in a day.* These words remind us that it takes time for things to happen, and usually, the more important something is, the more time it requires.

That shouldn't be a problem. Since we're good at doing tasks we can start and finish in one day, how hard can it be to do ones that don't produce immediate results? The answer is … harder than we think. Something happens when the connection between effort and accomplishment changes from immediate to some future date. Work becomes proportionally more difficult the further away it is from achievement. Play is the same way, too. I've known plenty of people who played tennis, basketball, golfed, swam, or biked, but I have never known anyone who ran marathons. That's because marathons require significant effort and training before you are ready to even begin competing in them.

One of the downsides of technological advancement is how it spoils us and creates an instant-gratification mentality. We push buttons or touch screens, and things happen immediately. We have trouble understanding why all of life can't be this way (there must be a "make it happen" app we can download!). With Rome, we are reminded that not everything can be instantly accomplished.

When society was largely agrarian, people possessed a mindset that enabled them to work patiently toward goals that were far beyond their horizon. Patience was built into their distant gratification way of life. You couldn't rush the seasons or speed up the growth cycle of crops or animals. As we left that world behind, we lost some of the ability to manage the often-daunting gulf between effort and achievement. As a result, we are more tempted to postpone working on something if the results are too far off. We often lack a sense of urgency and are content to live on cruise control. After all, what difference does it make if we take some time off? And while a Sabbath day's rest is a wonderful idea, a Sabbath lifestyle is not. Rome might not have been built in a day, but it was built daily.

A Message to the Corinthians

Paul is detailing his role in the ministry of reconciliation God had established through Jesus (2 Corinthians 5:11ff., esp. v. 18). This reaches a crescendo as he writes, "We speak for Christ when we plead, 'Come back to God!' For God made Christ, who never sinned, to be the offering for our sin, so that we could be made right with God through Christ" (vv. 20–21 *New Living Translation*). He then urges the Corinthians "not to receive God's grace in vain" for "now is the time of God's favor, today is the day of salvation" (6:1–2 NIV).

There were some at Corinth who needed to examine themselves to see whether they were in the faith (13:5), and these words would have certainly applied to their situation. But they probably had a broader application than that. To appreciate it, we need to understand that while there is a time when salvation initially takes place, it is a continuing aspect of our relationship with God and can be spoken of as past, present, or future (Romans 5:9–11). In other words, our salvation is ongoing. It is like the marriage relationship—although there is a specific time and place when a man and a woman became one as husband and wife, their oneness is a dynamic, recurring aspect of their relationship. In a healthy marriage, things are done every day that reflect this—they share conversational intimacies, affection, encouragement, prayer, and other things to renew their oneness.

In the same way, Paul's words are meant to make us realize our relationship with God is not something to be minimized, trivialized, or taken for granted. Instead, it is something to be appreciated and acted upon each day. Because of what God has accomplished through Jesus, "the new creation has come" (5:17—and it is not going anywhere!). Now is the time of His favor and the day of salvation. It is always the appropriate time for us to live in His salvation and be co-workers with Him in sharing His grace with others.

Words from Isaiah

Paul quotes an Old Testament text (Isaiah 49:8) to make his case for living daily in God's salvation. The passage is rooted in Israel's exile in Babylon (v. 8ff, v. 21) and concerns a "servant." The servant doesn't appear to be an individual, but rather the righteous remnant in Israel whom God was using and would use to reach the unrighteous of the nation as well as the rest of the world (vv. 5–6; and note Acts 13:46ff, where Paul applies Isaiah 49:6 to himself and Silas and their outreach to the Gentiles).

The servant had acted as God's messenger of judgment, telling of Israel's exile and the reason for it, but also speaking of their coming salvation (return from exile). Yet everything the servant said had been summarily rejected ("despised and abhorred by the nation" – v. 7). The servant felt he had "labored in vain" and spent his strength "for nothing at all" (v. 4). God assured him there would be a "time of My favor" and "a day of salvation" when he would receive help and be used to "restore the land and to reassign its desolate inheritances and to say to the captive, 'Come out,' and to those in darkness, 'Be free!'" (vv. 8–9).

Israel's deliverance from exile in Babylon pictures the greater salvation we have from sin through Christ, which Paul discussed in 2 Corinthians. There is never a need to feel we are laboring in vain or spending our strength on nothing—we live in the time of God's favor. Every day is a day of deliverance for the follower of Jesus. We are living in God's salvation.

Acting on the Opportunity

Paul's words do more than call us to make sure our relationship with God is healthy—there is an urgency in them. They challenge us to recognize now is the time to put our faith into action. Just as God's favor enabled the righteous remnant to fulfill their mission in Isaiah, His salvation means we are to be busy and active disciples. Whether it is being a co-worker with God in sharing His grace (6:1–2), severing ungodly relationships (6:14ff), pursuing holiness/wholeness (7:1), or sharing what we have with others (8:1ff), we are to live with a sense of urgency and industriousness. We are to seize the day and live with a sense of discipline in regard to the opportunities that are before us.

There's another facet we haven't touched on—being ready for the unplanned opportunity. Many of us are good at "planning the work and working the plan," but we sometimes stumble when it comes to those spontaneous moments that are part of everyone's life. Is there a way we can plan for the unplanned? Within reason, I think there is. It has to do with developing a mindset that is prepared for the unseen opportunity. There are three words that can get us started in that direction.

The first word is *aware*. Most of us start our day with some kind of plan that is a blend of what we have to do and what we hope to do. This is wise because it enables us to be more efficient and not waste time wondering what to do next. However, there is also the danger of becoming so fixated with our plan that we become oblivious to what is occurring around us. After all, opportunities rarely send announcements—they just happen. That's why we need to pay attention and be aware of what is happening around us. Recognizing this is a start, but it takes some discipline as well as diligence for most of us to remain focused and alert.

Steve Hartman of CBS News told a story about a 13-year-old boy in Michigan who was riding home on a school bus. Of all the students on the bus, he alone noticed that the driver was having a medical emergency. He got up from his seat and rushed to the front of the bus, grabbing the steering wheel and depressing the brake. His actions ensured the safety of other passengers and the driver, who later received medical attention. When

Hartman asked why the seventh-grader was the only one to notice what was happening, he found out all the other students were "engrossed in their electronics." The seventh-grader did not have a cell phone, and as his father later noted:

> What else are you going to do when you don't have a cell phone? You're going to look at people. You're going to notice stuff. You're going to look out the window and enjoy the world. It is a very powerful lesson. Maybe a change-the-world kind of lesson, I don't know.

To be clear, technology is not to blame; our failure to control technology is the problem. Immersing ourselves in our electronics (especially in public spaces) can blind us to opportunities. We should be looking, listening, and learning from the circumstances around us.

The next word is *authentic*. This is a word we hear quite often and in different contexts. If the first step is to be aware, the second is to consider how we should respond to an opportunity. This is the one most of us will find a little tricky. Not every opportunity we come across is meant for or right for us. After all, would you give a boat ride to Jonah or synagogue directions to Saul? An overly sensitive conscience might make us always want to jump into every situation—even when it is best not to or to let someone more qualified handle things. On the other hand, it is exceedingly easy for many of us to find reasons not to get involved. Being authentic means we ask God to help us see situations not as we are but as they are and act accordingly.

The last word is *adaptable* because that's what life calls us to be each day. We don't know what the day will hold, but we do know Who holds the day. Knowing that this is the time of His favor and the day of salvation, our schedule changes to now consist of this: what we have to do, what we want to do—and whatever might come up as we partner with our Father in dispensing His grace as we live in the now.

The word becoming flesh: Three habits have been quite helpful to me in learning to slow down and live in each day. One is praying before I get out of bed in the morning. I know from personal experience this carries the risk of going back to sleep, but the reward of asking for God's involvement in my day before my feet are on the floor far outweighs the risk for me. The second habit is cultivating the practice of being aware of what the date is. Granted, it is a small thing and doesn't do anything to slow down the rush of time, but it does make me feel like I lived through it instead of it being just a blur. The final habit is journal writing. I keep a record of what happened in the day and note special blessings. An added benefit of journaling is the ability to look back and reflect on these experiences (and my response to them) at a later time.

Living Within Our Limits

"Therefore do not worry about tomorrow, for tomorrow will worry about itself. Each day has enough trouble of its own." (Matthew 6:34)

Warren Wiersbe said, "No person, no matter how wealthy or gifted, can live two days at a time." Not only is that true, but there are other limitations we face regarding time and living. We can't relive yesterday or start tomorrow ahead of time. And while it is noble to struggle against things that masquerade as boundaries, it is not smart (or God-honoring) to bang our heads against walls of reality established by Him. Part of what it means to be human is being subject to certain limitations. In such cases, we must accept these and learn how to live within them.

While that's certainly part of what lies behind the words of Jesus when He tells us to focus on today instead of worrying about tomorrow, it is not the most important part. The ultimate basis for taking life one day at a time is because we trust our Father. It is interesting to note that Jesus spoke these words immediately after His instruction to "seek first His kingdom and His righteousness" (v. 33)—perhaps suggesting that what often gets in the way of true kingdom living is a failure to focus on the day at hand. Trying to live outside of today is tempting at times, but it is not how life is meant to be lived. What are some things that make it difficult for us to live within a day?

Up all Night

Jesus identified anxiety as an enemy of daily living (v. 34). Anxiety seems to be everywhere. Every day we hear reports, stories, and statistics about it. It is like the pandemic came along and took the lid off our anxiety jar, and everything started spilling out.

But that perception isn't entirely accurate. According to research conducted by The American Psychiatric Association and The U.K. Council for Psychotherapy in 2017, a third of respondents reported an increase in anxiety. The World Health Organization reported a 25% increase in anxiety and depression during the first year of the pandemic (2020). If you're keeping score, that's an almost 60% spike in four years! The U.S. Preventative Services Task Force recently recommended that everyone from 8 years and up be regularly screened for symptoms of anxiety. Speaking of our children, the U.S. Center for Disease Control and Prevention reported that almost 14% of our children have suffered from anxiety or depression, while *Medical News Today* told us that anxiety affects about 40 million people in the U.S.—almost 1 out of every 5 people. Anxiety is on the rise!

Anxiety can be triggered by hormonal or chemical imbalances, traumatic episodes, drug abuse, etc. (The CDC has been straightforward about the short-term and long-anxiety that marijuana can cause). However, even in such cases, there is often a spiritual element that can be a contributing factor and should not be overlooked. When you begin to consider the prevalence of anxiety in our culture, it is difficult not to think there is a correlation between the diminishment of faith and the surge in anxiety—especially among the younger generation. The Pew Research Center reports that 37% of older millennials (those born during the 80's) identified as "nones" (no religious affiliation). Meanwhile, 63% of younger millennials (those born during the 90s), identified as "nones." That's a sharp increase and means that roughly 50% of millennials aren't part of a church family. At least half of that number don't believe in God. If someone detaches themselves from the transcendent God and the encouragement and comfort that comes from being part of His people, should we really be surprised if they experience anxiety issues? I think we would be more surprised if they didn't.

When we are spiritually anxious or worried, we are worshiping at the wrong altar. Paul told Timothy that, "The Spirit God gave us does not make us timid, but gives us power, love and self-discipline" (2 Timothy 1:7). Spiritual anxiety occurs when we give too much attention to our circumstances and not enough to God. It is Peter dwelling on the wind and the waves. It is the army of Israel allowing Goliath to eclipse God Almighty. It is Martha frittering away in the presence of Jesus.

The people Jesus addressed in our text were not obsessing over trivial matters—He was talking to those who likely lived close to subsistence level. Their concerns were food, clothing, and shelter (Matthew 6:25ff). They would be tempted to see acquiring the ability to stockpile these things as the solution to their problems (6:19ff). Isn't that the way we usually think about it today? If we don't have enough, the solution is simple—we go get more, right?

This would be true if life consisted solely of material things and we were nothing more than animals. But the life our Father designed us for goes far beyond having full stomachs, clothes on our bodies, and a roof over our heads. We were made to image Him. We were made to love and be loved. Feeding, clothing, and sheltering our bodies will always be important, but it can never be ultimate. While having these things in abundance might be labeled by many as prosperity, to possess them apart from a relationship with our Father is, in reality, poverty. Having everything to live with is not the same as having something to live for, and in the end, isn't that what we really need?

Jesus wanted His listeners and us to understand that the central issue of life is this: Do we trust our Father? After all, while we are to take personal responsibility and work to obtain what we need (2 Thessalonians 3:10), it is idolatry (as we discussed in chapter 6) to fail to see God's presence in the process. Healthy responsibility can turn into heavy anxiety when this happens. He is the One who provides us with the strength and the ability to work. It is from His hand that seed comes for food and material for shelter. His care is witnessed by the world around us (Matthew 6:26–30). Therefore, the central issues of life are not resolved through worry, hurry, and scurry but by faith in God, who "daily bears our burdens" (Psalm 68:19). When anxiety comes calling, we need to turn it over to Him. After all, He's going to be up all night.

Thinking Big About the Small

Something else that can make it difficult to live within a day is our attitude about a day. As we observed in chapter two, with the exception of special days (holidays, birthdays, anniversaries, etc.), we tend to view a day as small, insignificant, and much too limiting. After all, we don't measure our age, anniversaries, or anything else we mark in time with days, weeks, or months—we do it in years because the other units are too little. That makes sense. Can you imagine someone telling you they are 10,950 days old? From a time-keeping perspective, days just aren't large enough to get the job done. What's true for marking time can be extended to many other things. A day is not big enough to:

o   change a habit
o   develop a meaningful relationship
o   build a house
o   take a vacation
o   teach someone to read
o   or write a book

When all is said and done, it is easy to see how a day can be reduced to relative insignificance. It might have been an acceptable unit of time for people who lived in simpler times centuries ago, but it has little place in our sophisticated world today. We live way too fast and too big for something so small. These words of Jesus can't apply to us today—can they?

It is important to realize in all this that thinking big isn't the enemy, any more than planning for the future (from a James 4:13–16 perspective) is. There's something healthy and important about seeing the big picture. The problem is rather "thinking small about the small," which is what we do when we diminish a day. The way we learn to live within a day is by thinking big about the small.

This isn't an unfamiliar concept. For example, you can take a small amount of money—the amount you might spend eating out and going to a movie—and put it into a savings account. If you did this every week over the course of a lifetime, you would end up with a significant amount of money thanks to compound interest. It would be much more than what you had put in. This could supplement your retirement benefits and enable you to be financially comfortable and generous to others, as well as make many other things possible. There are people who do this, and they illustrate this principle of thinking big about small things. While others think in small terms about their small amount of money, they look at that same small amount and envision great things. They think big about the small.

When Israel returned to their homeland in 538 BC, they began to rebuild the city of Jerusalem and the temple. When the foundation of the temple was laid, some of the older people wept because of its smallness compared to the much larger temple of Solomon they remembered (Ezra 3:12; Haggai 2:3). The prophet Zechariah told them not to "despise the day of small things" (4:10). In this, he was encouraging them to think big about the small. Great things were going to be associated with the temple (Haggai 2:6–9).

Few of us live lives filled with the big and spectacular. For the most part, our days are dominated by small things that seem to border on the trivial and are surely insignificant: doing whatever it is we do to pay the bills, keeping the home fires burning, squeezing in whatever else needs our attention, and then unwinding on the weekend so we can be ready to start it all over again on Monday. It is not as if we can draw a line from any of these things to anything notable or headline-worthy. It is just routine, everyday kind of stuff.

Or is it?

Do we mindlessly slog our way through these things, or do we intentionally offer them to our Father for His glory? Do we approach them with a hurry-up-and-get-it-over-with attitude, or do we offer up our best out of a spirit of service and love? Are we living in a conscientious way or unconsciously? The answers to these questions are important because they reveal whether we are *living* or *existing*. We're not really living life to its fullest until we've adopted the discipline of thinking big about each day of our lives.

This is very much a faith-based view of life. It is based on the belief that God does marvelous things with loaves and fishes, small stones, small steps (the walls of Jericho), and whatever else we put at His disposal. Seeing the seeds in an apple doesn't require much—just cut it open. But to think big about the small is to see the apple in the seeds, and that requires some faith.

Whether we're saving money, building temples, or just living life—let's make sure we see God in the details of living within each day.

The word becoming flesh: Learning to drink in life one day at a time requires some discernment on our part. Details inevitably pop into our lives every day and we must distinguish between those that are urgent and those that are important. Sometimes, it is the difference between something good and something better. Jesus and His disciples were graciously invited into Martha's home. She understandably felt an urgency about attending to the details of hospitality (something good), that caused her to overlook the importance of sitting at Jesus' feet and listening to Him (something better).

The God Who Bears Our Burdens

Praise be to the Lord, to God our Savior, who daily bears our burdens.
(Psalm 68:19)

When I was in college, I had a job with a company called Scientific Industries. Although that sounds kind of glamorous and high-tech, it was actually a cleaning services company where I did janitorial work. It was the kind of work not many people wanted to do, but it was a job—and I needed one! Although I ended up being the janitor at a plant that manufactured motherboards for touch tone phones, my initial job with them was (briefly) working on an all-night clean-up crew.

The all-night clean-up crew consisted of a handful of people who rode in a van that made several stops throughout the city—at banks, offices, and even a television station. As soon as the van pulled into the parking lot, we hopped out and immediately got to work. We did "spot cleaning,"—which meant we would vacuum high-traffic areas, empty trashcans, wipe down a few surfaces, and then get back in the van and head to the next place. I'm sorry to say that I no longer remember the name of the man who supervised our crew, but I will never forget that he was the hardest worker among us. We all looked up to him because he rolled up his sleeves and worked with us. We felt like he understood whatever we were going through because he wasn't sitting out in the van or taking it easy at a desk somewhere—he was right there with us.

As we come to the end of our journey together of considering how to live within a day for God, I know of no better place to finish than with the truth mentioned in passing in the first chapter from Psalm 68:19 about how God "daily bears our burdens." In the context of our discussion about living within the day for God, v. 19 lets us know that God has already been doing that for us! The One who created and sustains planets, solar systems, and galaxies daily bears our burdens, or, as ESV has it, "daily bears us up." This is what we need to know! Our Father isn't a far-off, detached spectator to our struggles or successes but Someone who enters into our circumstances and shares in them.

A Deeper Look

In Psalm 68, God is celebrated as a conquering king. In the first part of the psalm (vv. 7–18), He leads His people "from Sinai into His sanctuary" (v. 17). He goes "out before His people" (v. 7), cutting a swath through the wilderness and into the promised land of Canaan, scattering kings along the way (v. 14).

In the second half of the psalm (v. 24–27), He is enthroned in the sanctuary ("the procession of my God and King into the sanctuary," v. 24). The psalmist paints a festive scene involving singers, musicians, tribes, and princes (v. 25–27).

Before each of these sections, there is a call for God to be praised. Before the first section, we are told to "sing to God" (v. 4), who is described as "a father to the fatherless, a defender of widows" . . . One who "sets the lonely in families" and "leads out the prisoners with singing" (vv. 5–6). Before the second section, it is "Praise be to the Lord, to God our Savior" (v. 19). He goes on to say in v. 21 that "Our God is a God who saves, from the Sovereign Lord comes escape from death." Sandwiched in between these two truths is his characterization of God as One who "daily bears our burdens" (v. 19).

In the context of the psalm, these statements provided Israel with the reason for praise and rejoicing—their conquering King was unlike any other king—not just in power but, more importantly, in character and compassion! This was evidenced by His concern for the powerless (the fatherless, widows, and prisoners).

Just as everyone on our work crew found encouragement from our supervisor working by our side, we should find it immeasurably comforting and encouraging in living within the day for God and knowing He is doing the same for us. He knows us intimately and loves us ultimately.

While this is certainly a liberating truth, it is also a much-needed reminder that everything we offer to our Father is ultimately a response to all He has done, is doing, and will do for us. Our relationship with God is not a relationship of equals in either nature or giving. He is the Creator, and we are the created. He is also the Giver who can't be outgiven. He gives us life (1 Timothy 6:17). Then He gives us new life through Jesus. We receive forgiveness, the Spirit, and a ready-made spiritual family in the rich fellowship of the church. All of this points toward living eternally with Him when this life is over.

We can't out give God, but we don't have to. We can appreciate and enjoy His gifts, share them with others, and live in a responsive way toward Him. That is how we need to frame living within a day—as our grateful response to our loving, faithful Father.

Seeing This in Scripture

God's daily bearing of people's burdens isn't a truth that began with the psalmist—it is something we witness throughout the biblical record. In Genesis 3:15, God promised to "crush" the serpent's head. This refers to what Jesus would one day accomplish at the cross when He came "to destroy the devil's work" (1 John 3:8, Hebrews 2:14–17). Based on what would happen, God forgave people and lifted their burden of sin daily (see Romans 3:25–26).

It was an arduous, demanding journey as Israel trekked through the wilderness under Moses' leadership. They were tested in terms of their endurance. For forty years, they experienced a primitive, often hostile environment coupled with unrelenting tent living. They were challenged by the sameness of routine with little change in their circumstances or surroundings.

But God was with them each day and every step of the way. His continued presence was manifested by the cloud during the day and the fire at night. He provided manna for them, giving them enough on the sixth day so that they didn't need to gather any on the Sabbath. He raised up leaders for them in Moses, Aaron, Joshua, and others. In all of this, He was daily bearing their burdens!

The same thing was true for a group of people traveling through a different kind of wilderness. These were those who were part of the churches we read about from Acts through Revelation. They faced their own set of challenges. Because they accepted Jesus as the Messiah, they initially experienced persecution from many in the Jewish community. Later, as churches spread throughout the Roman Empire, disciples were often ostracized and viewed with suspicion by civil authorities and others because of their belief in Jesus as Lord (as opposed to Caesar). They often had to schedule their meetings for strange times and in secluded places (like the catacombs). But God bore the burdens of His people and blessed them.

Chronologically Distant, Spiritually Close

Of course, we are separated by not just centuries but millennia from the people we read about in the biblical witness. Because of this, it can be easy to feel disconnected from them and their stories, but we must fight this temptation. Just as Jesus showed absolutely no hesitation in speaking from Exodus (a book written approximately 1,500 years before the time He lived on earth) in defending the resurrection in Matthew 22:23–33, we should feel the same about these texts that assure us that God is with His people.

While the biblical narrative might be chronologically distant, it is spiritually close. It features men and women who, like us, sought to live for God. They faced challenges and obstacles as we do. In Scripture, we see how God continually brought them through whatever their trials were. Throughout the centuries, countless people have found strength in their stories because there is no expiration date for inspiration. "The word of God is living and active" (Hebrews 4:12).

Paul follows Jesus in pointing us to the value of ancient words:

For everything that was written in the past was written to teach us, so that through the endurance taught in the Scriptures and the encouragement they provide we might have hope. (Romans 15:4)

While we've focused on the importance of living within the day in this book, it is almost always easier to see the work of God in our lives by stepping back and looking at the bigger picture rather than by trying to parse out how He might have worked in a single day. In analytical terms, we can't see the forest for the trees. Like holding a book up to your face, we're too close to the situation to see what we're looking for. However, when we look back over a period of time or even the entirety of our lives, it is impossible not to see our Father's loving hand guiding us. Our stories then take their place with those we read about in the Bible, and we join with the psalmist in saying:

> We will tell the next generation the praiseworthy deeds of the LORD,
> his power, and the wonders he has done. (Psalm 78:4)

The word becoming flesh: Knowing God, the Creator and Sustainer of the universe, is with us and at work in our daily lives is an enabling truth we need to carry with us wherever we go and in whatever we do. How do we do this? There are reminders from Scripture we can commit to heart (texts like Psalm 23, 139:1–18; Hebrews 13:5–6). Prayer of any kind (written, spoken, silent) also reminds us of His presence. Worship with God's people—looking upward together is also a powerful affirmation of God's presence among us. ("The house of the Lord" references in Psalms bear witness to this truth).

Afterword

We began this book with a scenario about Lazarus's life after Jesus brought him back from the dead. We imagined him struggling to keep his faith fresh, his focus clear, and his feet on the ground every day.

But what if that hypothetical was totally off base? What if, post-resurrection, Lazarus knew how to live within a day? After all, no one would be in a better position to appreciate life than him. Suppose he decided to view each day as a bonus and see it for the incredible gift it was. Furthermore, he resisted the temptation to think of any day as a down payment on countless more. He simply celebrated each day as it was given, living with the wisdom that whether he received any more or not, each day was a unique entity. He found joy in it and greater joy in the One who gave it. If he lived this way, he truly honored the second chance at life he had received from Jesus.

This is how we want to live as disciples who have received our second chance, and I hope this book has been helpful toward that end. Living within the day keeps us rooted in God's grace and grounded in humility. Learning to look at a night's rest, strength for a day's work, and food for our bodies, as given by our Father, makes us aware of His daily presence in our lives and, more importantly, our presence in His life. It was Robert Louis Stevenson who said, "Anyone can carry his burden, however hard, until nightfall. Anyone can do his work, however hard, for one day. Anyone can live sweetly, patiently, lovingly, purely till the sun goes down. And this is all that life really means."

The totality of our lives is expressed in terms of a day. Each one is like a note in a song or a word in a book. Alone they may not seem like much, and yet if you leave just one of them out, the song or story is no longer the same.

Be proud and purposeful of each note and each word. Allow our Father to make something special of them. There's no day wasted when you live this way. Then, sometime in the future, life as we know it will be eclipsed by life as God knows it; time will yield to eternity, and "what is mortal" will "be swallowed up by life" (2 Corinthians 5:4).

Until then, let's live within each day for Him!

It may be that you don't have a relationship with God through Jesus. If this is the case, I'd encourage you to read the book of Acts. In it you'll find the accounts of men and women responding in faith to the good news of Jesus' death, burial, and resurrection for our sins through repentance, confession (Romans 10:9–10), and baptism.

It is an extraordinary picture that is painted. Thousands are baptized in Jerusalem on Pentecost. Jewish and Gentile households hear the good news, believe it, and are immersed. A person traveling through the desert on his way home to Ethiopia is taught about Christ and baptized. A merchant, a jailer—even someone who had practiced sorcery—they all had their sins forgiven, received the gift of the Holy Spirit, and found new life through Jesus.

This life can be yours when you respond as they did. It is my prayer that you will experience the abundant life that is in Him.

Questions

Chapter 1 — In The Beginning

1. Have you ever thought about God's design in reference to a day? Why or why not?
2. How would you describe the role of a day in the creation account of Genesis 1:1—2:3? Why was it important?
3. Is there anything in the creation narrative to suggest God was anxious or in a hurry? What does this say to us?
4. How do Exodus 20:8–11 and Mark 2:27 help us to see that God created a day with man in mind? Why is this important?
5. What is meant by the statement, "The currency God favors is a day?" Do you agree with this? Why or why not?

Chapter 2 — The Undervalued Asset

1. Can you think of a specific way the Scripture has challenged your thinking or changed your mind about something? What was it?
2. What is the difference between a day's relative and intrinsic values? Do you tend to think about a day's value more in one way than the other? If so, why do you think that is true?
3. Is it easy or difficult for you to approach each day as being priceless? Why?
4. What are ways we might trivialize a day?
5. What are some of the positive things that can happen when we see each day as a unique gift from God that is alive to all sorts of possibilities?

Chapter 3 — *Carpe Diem*

1. In what ways is Ecclesiastes different from most of the other books of the Bible?
2. What are the *carpe diem* passages, and what should we learn from them?
3. What is involved in receiving "God's gifts for what they are?
4. What is something you can do to help yourself live within the day?
5. What can we do to make sure we don't love our blessings more than God?

Chapter 4 — Daily Rejoicing

1. How does Psalm 118 begin and end? What does this indicate about the psalm?
2. How was Israel rejected by Egypt? Babylon?
3. How do the words of Psalm 118:22, "the stone the builders rejected has become the cornerstone," apply to Jesus? How do we know this?
4. How is God a God of reversal? What does this mean to us?
5. How can the truths of this psalm help us to live gloriously ever after?

Chapter 5 — Community Watch

1. Why is community so important to us? Can you think of a time in your life when you were made especially aware of this truth?
2. What is the context of the Hebrews letter? How does it relate to your life?
3. Why is courage needed to live as a disciple of Jesus?
4. What does it do for you when someone offers encouragement? What does it do for you when you give encouragement? Why do you think it is more blessed to give than to receive?
5. What is the greatest challenge you face in being an encourager?

Chapter 6 — Daily Bread

1. Why do you think asking God for our daily bread is important? Is this a challenge for you? Why or why not?
2. Why do you think Jesus included this in the Model Prayer? How does it fit in with the rest of the prayer?
3. Why is it important to not think of our Father as a "God of the gaps"?
4. Why does explaining how something works scientifically not make God "unnecessary?"
5. Jeremiah could see God's goodness and provision even in a time of extreme adversity. Are we? Which is the greater challenge for you: adversity or prosperity? Why?

Chapter 7 — Not By Bread Alone

1. How would your spiritual life be affected if someone took away your Bible (and all access to Scripture)?
2. What would you say was the role of Scripture in bringing people into a relationship with God?

3. What is the significance of Jesus telling Satan that "man shall not live on bread alone, but on every word that comes from the mouth of God?" In what other ways did He demonstrate the importance of God's word?
4. Is it spiritual to pursue God through the Scripture? Why or why not? Why were the Bereans praised by God through Luke?
5. Is it more accurate to think of the Bible as a vast collection of verses or a smaller collection of books? Why? What are some benefits of reading the Bible book by book?

Chapter 8 — Wear It or Bear It?

1. How would you put what Jesus said in Luke 9:23 into your own words? What are some specific ways this is shaping your life?
2. How was the cross fundamental to Jesus' identity? How is it fundamental to ours?
3. How is it that we find life when we give ours up to God? Why do you think more people don't do this? How can we help them?
4. What does it mean to live with open hands?
5. In what ways is discipleship like living at the airport? What are some of the challenges of airport living?

Chapter 9 — Blessed Are the Grinders

1. What percentage of your life is devoted to work? How much is "free time"? Are you tempted to think that serving God takes place only during your "free time"? Why or why not?
2. Of the different texts mentioned in this piece, which one speaks to you the most about the importance of the work we do? Are there other passages (not mentioned here) that are helpful?
3. Which do you think is more important: what we do or how we do it? Why?
4. How is God using your work? Does being unable to answer that (to your complete satisfaction) mean that it isn't being used? What does it mean?
5. Which of the four statements at the end of the chapter do you find to be most helpful? Why?

Chapter 10 — Get Yourself Renewed

1. In what way did Paul not compare favorably with some self-appointed apostles the Corinthians had come into contact with? Was this a valid point? Do we see this type of thinking today?

2. Can you think of some examples of our culture's youth infatuation? How is this harmful at an individual level? Societal level?
3. What is a healthy, biblical way to look at aging?
4. How would you put together the truths of 2 Corinthians 3:18 and 4:16? See if you can come up with your own paraphrase.
5. What are some practical ways we can focus less on the flesh and more on the things that are unseen?

Chapter 11 — Living in the New

1. How well do you handle the gap between effort and achievement? Would you describe yourself as a person of patience and persistence?
2. How has technology shaped us in terms of expecting instant gratification? What are some ways we can restore some balance?
3. How is it that the "day of salvation" Paul speaks of is a time to be active rather than passive? In what ways did he call upon the Corinthians to be active?
4. Why is "every day is a day of salvation" for the disciple?
5. Three concepts are discussed at the close of the chapter that help us deal with unexpected opportunities: awareness, authenticity, and adaptability. Which of these is your strength? Which is your weakness?

Chapter 12 — Living Within Our Limits

1. How is learning to live within a day a faith response? What suggestion is made about it as it relates to "seeking first His kingdom and His righteousness?"
2. In what ways can anxiety negatively affect us? How can it keep us from living one day at a time?
3. What role do you think our faith has in helping us overcome our anxieties and fears?
4. Is thinking big about the small a challenge for you? Why or why not? How does this relate to daily living?
5. What is the biggest challenge you face in living within a day?

Chapter Thirteen/The God Who Bears Our Burdens

1. In what ways does it help you to hear the truth that God "daily bears our burdens?" Does it surprise you that God does this? Why or why not?

2. What do you think might be the significance of this truth being presented to us in connection with God's sovereignty in Psalm 68?

3. Israel traversing through the wilderness and the opposition faced by the early church were two examples of God bearing the burdens of His people. What are some others you can think of?

4. What does it mean to speak of the biblical witness as chronologically distant but spiritually close?

5. In what ways can you see God's work in your life? How does this encourage you?

A Selected Bibliography

Brooks, David. *The Second Mountain,* Random House, 2019.

Dillard, Raymond B. and Trevor Longman III. *Ecclesiastes: An Introduction to the Old Testament,* Zondervan Publishing House, 1994.

Gordon, Arthur. *A Touch of Wonder,* Guidepost Associates, Inc., 1974.

Harris, Murray, *2 Corinthians, The Expositors Bible Commentary (Revised Edition),* Zondervan, 2008.

Krznaric, Roman, *Carpe Diem: Seizing the Day in a Distracted World,* Penguin Random House LLC, 2017.

Lewis, C. S, *Mere Christianity,* HarperOne, 2000.

Lindbergh, Anne Morrow, Gift from the Sea, Pantheon Books, 1975.

Mays, James Luther. *Psalms: Interpretation—A Bible Commentary for Preaching and Teaching,* John Know Press, 1994.

McKelvey, Douglas, *Every Moment Holy (Volume 1),* Rabbit Room Press, 2017.

McGuiggan, Jim, Spending Time with Jim McGuiggan, *JimMcGuiggan. Wordpress.com/,* 2016.

Scott, James M., *2 Corinthians, Understanding the Bible Commentary Series,* Baker Books, 1998.

Shepherd, Jerry E., *Ecclesiastes, The Expositor's Bible Commentary (Revised Edition),* Zondervan, 2008.

Tiede, David L., *Luke—Augsburg Commentary on the New Testament,* Augsburg Publishing House, 1988.

www.ingramcontent.com/pod-product-compliance
Lightning Source LLC
LaVergne TN
LVHW010318070426
835508LV00033B/3496